MW01133493

Hal Ashby: Interviews

Conversations with Filmmakers Series
Peter Brunette, General Editor

Hal Ashby

INTERVIEWS

Edited by Nick Dawson

University Press of Mississippi / Jackson

www.upress.state.ms.us

The University Press of Mississippi is a member of the Association of American University Presses.

Copyright © 2010 by University Press of Mississippi
All rights reserved
Manufactured in the United States of America

First printing 2010
Library of Congress Cataloging-in-Publication Data

Hal Ashby : interviews / edited by Nick Dawson.
        p. cm. — (Conversations with filmmakers series)
    Includes filmography and index.
    ISBN 978-1-60473-564-2 (cloth : alk. paper) — ISBN 978-1-60473-565-9 (pbk. : alk.
paper) 1. Ashby, Hal—Interviews. 2. Motion picture producers and directors—United
States—Interviews. I. Dawson, Nick, 1980–
    PN1998.3.A7635H35 2010
    791.4302'33092—dc22   2009049312

British Library Cataloging-in-Publication Data available

Contents

Introduction

In 2003, I went into one of the best film bookstores in London armed with a list of movies I was researching. I showed it to the clerk behind the counter and asked if he could suggest any books that would be helpful. While he considered my question, he commented on those movies on the list that he had seen, which was most of them.

Then he paused and said, "I'm intrigued—what's the connection between all these films?"

"They're all by Hal Ashby," I said.

During the years I spent researching *Being Hal Ashby: Life of a Hollywood Rebel*, the first and so far only biography of Hal Ashby, I frequently thought back on this incident. Ashby, it seemed, was the forgotten man of the New Hollywood generation. "I know that name . . . " people would often say when I mentioned I was working on an Ashby biography. And then, "Remind me, what films did he direct?" But when I mentioned his movies, people's eyes generally lit up: *Harold and Maude* and *Being There* are probably the most recognizable and beloved, but *Shampoo* and *Coming Home* are also popular favorites. *The Last Detail* and *Bound for Glory* are well-loved too, and true cinephiles will talk excitedly about *The Landlord*, Ashby's criminally underseen debut. In fact, Hal Ashby's films of the 1970s are considered some of the best and most important of their era, yet as a director he remains relatively unknown and unacknowledged.

The question that naturally arises is "Why?" While there's no one explanation, a number of significant factors have led to Ashby being consigned to relative obscurity after his death. In his 1970 book *The Film Director as Superstar*, Joseph Gelmis wrote, "The director is in vogue today," and maintained that "the phenomenon will not soon peak and pass."[1] In the decade that followed, his prediction was borne out. During the New Hollywood era, the director was king and auteurs with outsized personalities and ballooning egos thrived: Francis Ford Coppola, Peter Bogdanovich, William Friedkin, Martin Scorsese, Robert Altman, Brian De Palma, and Bob Rafelson, not to mention the inventors of the blockbuster, Steven Spielberg and George Lucas. As the old Hollywood collapsed and a fresh one replaced it, a film's director became just as important as its stars had once been.

In the midst of this group of self-promoting, hyperconfident directors was Hal Ashby, a man who, for all his self-assurance and talent, left his ego at the door and put the work first. The universal story you will hear from people who worked with Ashby is that he was the most democratic of directors, who would just as readily listen to an idea from a grip as a suggestion from his cinematographer, writer, or lead actor. When Ashby worked on *The Big Country* (1958) as an assistant editor, that film's director, William Wyler, had told him, "Whenever you have any ideas about anything, please get them out some way." A hippie before the word was invented, Ashby believed in the collaborative nature of filmmaking and took Wyler's philosophy to heart, applying it later in his own work as a director.

This was particularly true with actors, who thrived under Ashby's direction—or lack of. Ashby extended great freedom to his actors; he never tried to alter or influence their performance, but instead made it clear that he had complete faith in their abilities. The performances in Ashby's movies were, as a result, vital, genuine, and immediate, and his films from the 1970s received eleven Academy Award nominations for acting. Ironically, this had the effect of taking the focus away from Ashby's contribution to the film.

While beloved by his actors and crew, Ashby drew little attention from the film press; his first few films weren't very successful, and when he had box office hits—with such films as *Shampoo, Coming Home*, and *Being There*—the credit was often ascribed to the stars of those movies. What's more, Ashby was not making movies that could be easily lumped together—what, for example, was the connective tissue between the political focus and documentary-like realism of *Coming Home* and the hippie philosophizing and quaint absurdism of *Harold and Maude?*—and accordingly, unlike many of his peers, he wasn't seen as an auteur. Andrew Sarris, the American critic who was the major proponent of the auteur theory in the U.S., declared in 1976, "Ashby interests me, but I have not completely figured out his style."[2]

But perhaps the most important factor in the decline of the public's perception of Ashby was the string of critical and box office failures that defined his post-1970s directing career.

In the fall of 1982, Dale Pollock, the then-editor of the *Los Angeles Times'* Calendar section, wrote a profile entitled "Whatever Happened to Hal Ashby?" Ashby's marketing guru, Mike Kaplan, was friendly with Pollock and had assured Ashby—who had not conducted an interview in over two years—that the article would be sympathetic to him. Kaplan said that Pollock was "a fan (saw *Being There* four times) and can be trusted."[3] The piece was, however, a hatchet job that focused on the decline of Ashby's career; to make it worse, it was coupled with a picture of Ashby—taken just as he had removed his glasses and was trying to refocus his eyes—looking strung out.

The question in the title of Pollock's article, though, was a good one. Peter Biskind, in his seminal account of the New Hollywood generation, *Easy Riders, Raging Bulls*, says that Ashby "had the most remarkable run of any '70s director,"[4] yet just two years after the end of the 1970s, Ashby was perceived as a spent force. So, whatever did happen to Hal Ashby?

The story that went around Hollywood was that, as Biskind puts it, Ashby "disappeared into the dark tunnel of post-'70s, Me Decade drugs and paranoia." It was a very neat explanation; the only problem was that it wasn't true. Ashby was Hollywood's hippie poster child, a man who had directed *Harold and Maude* with a beard that strayed well below his shoulders, who had declared, "I was so loaded on that film, I could hardly walk,"[5] and had been arrested at Toronto International Airport for possession of marijuana shortly after *Harold and Maude's* release. However, after this he had trimmed his beard and generally smartened up his image. Though he remained a daily pot smoker and—like so many others in Hollywood at the time—dabbled with cocaine, it seemed that his run of successes would not stop. Until the end of the decade, that is.

In 1978, Ashby signed a three-picture deal with Lorimar, the TV production company behind *The Waltons* and *Eight Is Enough*, planning to make his first two Lorimar movies back-to-back, and then edit them simultaneously. In the fall of 1982, the last of those three movies, *Lookin' To Get Out*, was finally released after almost two years in the editing room: Ashby's dealings with Lorimar had been very troubled, post-production periods had been agonizingly protracted, and cutting multiple movies simultaneously had ultimately not worked out as he had planned. Ashby's fractious relationship with Lorimar had lead to word going around town that he was a washed-up junkie, unable to finish a movie, a liability. In the very different environment of 1980s Hollywood—where a film's commercial prospects now took precedence over creative concerns—this was exactly the opposite of what the studios were looking for in a director.

Ashby was, in fact, not a junkie, but a workaholic and a perfectionist who had long used work as a buffer or distraction from the problems of his personal life. Juggling multiple movies suited him but not Lorimar's executives, who were anxious to see Ashby and his keen but inept rookie editing crews create releasable versions of the problematic *Second Hand Hearts* and *Lookin' To Get Out*. As time wore on and tensions grew, the anti-authoritarian Ashby responded to Lorimar's increasingly aggressive actions by locking himself away and trying to avoid or ignore the conflict. Drugs were neither the root nor any real part of the frictions between him and Lorimar, but ultimately his image as a hippie, an unrepentant pot smoker and a loose cannon gave his employers an easy out.

Ashby's career started to go wrong when he signed on with Lorimar, but his slide continued after they parted company. Lorimar blocked him from making *Tootsie*, the film that would have been his follow-up to *Lookin' To Get Out*—on a contractual technicality—but then bafflingly let him direct the Rolling Stones concert movie *Let's Spend the Night Together*, which had only limited success. His final two features, *The Slugger's Wife* (1985) and *8 Million Ways to Die* (1986), were—like *Lookin' To Get Out*—taken away from him in the editing room, despite the fact that he was an Academy Award–winning editor. Not surprisingly, they were critical and commercial failures.

The commonly held perception of the end of Ashby's life is that *8 Million Ways to Die* was the final nail in his coffin, that Hollywood wanted nothing further from him, and that he died shortly after. (Some accounts I have read even state that he died of a drug overdose.) In fact, Ashby separated himself from Hollywood rather than vice versa, taking time out to develop his own projects on his own terms and schedule. In 1988, he was lining up a trio of literary adaptations—movie versions of Truman Capote's *Handcarved Coffins*, Thomas Berger's *Vital Parts*, and Richard Brautigan's *The Hawkline Monster*—when he discovered he had untreatable pancreatic cancer.

Ashby died on December 27, 1988; like many others who have passed away during the holiday period, his death got relatively little attention. His memorial at the Directors Guild of America building was well attended by Hollywood's great and good, and those who were away in Aspen or Vail skiing with their families sent on messages to be read out. In the major newspapers, he received short and respectful obituaries which typically underlined the contributions of his collaborators when explaining the success of so many of his films. The picture they painted was of a force long spent, an overrated talent whose favor had run out, and who was now ready to be forgotten.

During the period of time when I was researching and writing my biography of Ashby, there was a noticeable shift. His collaborators and contemporaries had always spoken highly of him, but now the generation of filmmakers who had grown up watching his movies joined them. Alexander Payne spoke of his love of Ashby and the influence of *The Landlord* on *Sideways*, while Wes Anderson raved about *Harold and Maude* (which he references in *Rushmore*) and said that *Shampoo* was his favorite movie. Both Cameron Crowe and Judd Apatow, two directors who shared with Ashby a passion for music as well as cinema, talked repeatedly about their love of his movies. When *Thumbsucker* and *Rocket Science* were released, their respective directors, Mike Mills and Jeffrey Blitz, seemingly mentioned Ashby in every interview they gave, and the screenwriters of *Away We Go*, Dave Eggers and Vendela Vida, also spoke enthusiastically and often about the importance of Ashby to their movie. *Little Miss Sunshine*'s writer-directors Valerie Faris and Jonathan Dayton namechecked him as an influence, as did *Half Nelson*'s creative team, Ryan Fleck and Anna Boden. George Clooney, Zach Braff, Steven Soderbergh, Darren Aronofsky, Noah Baumbach, Spike Jonze, and Miranda July have also all gone on record as Ashby fans. In my own work interviewing directors for *Filmmaker* magazine over the last few years, I have been amazed and heartened to find that (without any prompting on my part) Ashby's name crops up more often than any other as an inspiration to young auteurs.

In 2008, *Good* magazine published an article on the very subject of Ashby's popularity among the present generation of filmmakers entitled "The Director's Director." In it, a group of directors and writers each contributed short essays on one of Ashby's movies: Alexander Payne wrote on *The Landlord*, Jason Schwartzman on *Harold and Maude*, Wes Anderson on *The Last Detail*, David O. Russell on *Shampoo*, and Judd Apatow on *Being There*.

Apatow's piece begins as follows: "When I was asked to write about the film *Being There*, I thought it would be fun. I am a big fan of Hal Ashby's work, and *Being There* has always been one of my favorite films. I thought it would be a blast. I quickly realized that I had not seen the film in a long time and that I probably should watch it again so I could refresh my memory. That was my mistake. After watching it again I got very depressed. It was even better than I remembered it to be. Fuck this article. Sometimes seeing a great film takes the wind out of you. Watching this film reminded me how far I have to go."[6]

And maybe that's why Ashby is so important once again. In a time when Hollywood is more focused on car chases and explosions than character and exposition, Ashby's movies provide a perfect counterpoint. They are stories about people, told with humanity and humor. They tackle big subjects with a light touch. They are edgy and subversive. They have great scripts, memorable performances, subtle directing. They were made within the system, but reflect an outsider's view. For contemporary filmmakers looking back, Ashby's movies are an example of what Hollywood cinema once was and, they hope, could be again.

Ashby's renaissance gained even more momentum in 2009: not only was *Being Hal Ashby: Life of Hollywood Rebel* published, but Ashby's previously undiscovered director's cut of *Lookin' To Get Out* was released on DVD, Ashby retrospectives and tribute events were organized by both the Academy of Motion Picture Arts and Sciences and the Sarasota Film Festival, and a critical work, *The Films of Hal Ashby* by Christopher Beach, also came out.

And now, in the wake of all that, this book, which I hope will help in the greater cause of restoring Hal Ashby to his proper place in the cinematic pantheon. Over the course of his twenty-year career as a film director, Ashby was interviewed less frequently than one might have expected given the success of his films. (There is, for example, only one interview about *Shampoo* that I can locate.) However, as a subject he was always forthcoming, interesting, and generous, and as a result the Q&As and profiles in this book are of a particularly high standard. The first piece is "Breaking Out of the Cutting Room," an article about *The Landlord* and Ashby's years before he became a director which was most likely ghost written for Ashby by a journalist from *Action* magazine, the official publication of the Directors Guild of America. And closing out the book is the fascinating and very revealing "How to Kill a Movie," an oral history piece written by Ashby's friend Michael Dare which lays bare the numerous difficulties—including Ashby's firing—on his final film, *8 Million Ways to Die.*

I am very grateful to Leila Salisbury—who was briefly my editor on *Being Hal Ashby* before moving on to the University Press of Mississippi—for asking me to edit this volume. I also want to thank all the writers, publishers, institutions, and individuals who granted me permission to reprint these interviews, especially those who so generously waived or lowered their fees. Lastly, and always, I must thank Heather, my wife, constant companion, and personal copy editor, who kicks my sloppy sentences into shape and gives greater meaning to my words, just as she does to my life.

ND

Notes

1. Joseph Gelmis, *The Film Director as Superstar* (New York: Doubleday and Company, 1970), ix.

2. Andrew Sarris "Our Critic Eyes the Future and Blinks," *Village Voice*, September 13, 1976, 107.

3. Nick Dawson, *Being Hal Ashby: Life of a Hollywood Rebel* (Lexington: University Press of Kentucky, 2009), 268.

4. Peter Biskind, *Easy Riders, Raging Bulls: How the Sex 'N' Drugs 'N' Rock 'N' Roll Generation Saved Hollywood* (London: Bloomsbury, 1998) 170.

5. Dawson, *Being Hal Ashby*, 120.

6. Jennifer Wachtell, "The Director's Director," *Good*, Issue 11, June 1998 (http://www .good.is/post/the_directors_director/).

Chronology

1929	Born William Hal Ashby on September 2, in Ogden, Utah, to James Thomas Ashby and Eileen Hetzler Ashby. He is the youngest of four children, coming after two brothers, "Hetz" (b. 1910) and Jack (b. 1925), and a sister, Ardith (b. 1912).
1935	Parents divorce.
1936	Father marries Clarissa Little.
1942	Father dies, ostensibly having committed suicide.
1945	Is sent by mother to the Puget Sound Naval Academy (PSNA) for high school.
1947	Marries Lavon Compton in March, and then returns to PSNA to finish high school. In September, his daughter, Leigh Ashby, is born.
1948	Leaves Ogden and begins divorce proceedings with Lavon. After hitchhiking around the Pacific Northwest, he ends up in Los Angeles.
1949	Marries Maxine Armstrong; they divorce soon afterwards.
1950–1955	Is part of bohemian group of young men living in Los Angeles, including Bill Box, Bill Otto, Ian Bernard, and John Mandel. He develops an interest in directing and is told that editing is the best route to achieving that goal.
1956	Is hired on the B-movie *The Naked Hills* as an assistant editor. Meets and marries Maloy "Mickey" Bartron.
1957	Gains membership in the Society of Motion Picture Film Editors, and gets assistant editing job on *The Big Country*, working under Robert Swink.
1958	Writes first screenplay, *The Sound of Silence*, with Ian Bernard.
1958–1964	Works as Swink's protégé on all his films, including George

Stevens's *The Diary of Anne Frank* (1959) and William Wyler's *The Children's Hour* (1961).

1959–1960   Makes unsuccessful move to Europe with Mickey.

1960   Mickey leaves him for John Barreto, whom she later marries.

1961   Mickey begins divorce proceedings against Ashby. Ashby falls in love with Shirley Citron, another editor, who is already pregnant. Her daughter, Carrie, is born later that year and given the last name Ashby.

1963   Marries Shirley after the final dissolution of his marriage to Mickey.

1964   Is promoted to editor on *The Greatest Story Ever Told*, but quits to cut *The Loved One* for Tony Richardson, a job which is short-lived. Norman Jewison hires him to edit *The Cincinnati Kid*; it is the beginning of a fruitful creative partnership and a close friendship.

1966   Edits *The Russians Are Coming, The Russians Are Coming* for Jewison, for which he and co-editor J. Terry Williams are nominated for an Academy Award. Is also given role of assistant to producer on the film by Jewison.

1967   Edits Jewison's *In the Heat of the Night*, on which he is also associate producer. Separates from Shirley.

1968   Wins Academy Award for Best Editing for *In the Heat of the Night*. Edits *The Thomas Crown Affair*, on which he is also associate producer. Ashby and Shirley divorce, with the final rift in their marriage occurring on the day their adoption of Steven Ashby, a young mixed-race boy, is finalized.

1969   Makes his directorial debut on *The Landlord*, based on Kristin Hunter's novel and starring Beau Bridges and Lee Grant. Marries actress Joan Marshall (the mother of teenagers Sheri and Stephen Marshall) on the set of the film. Jewison's *Gaily, Gaily*, on which Ashby is associate producer but not editor, is released.

1970   *The Landlord* is released to good reviews and modest business. Lee Grant is nominated for Best Supporting Actress. Ashby and Joan divorce, but continue to have an on-off relationship.

1971   Shoots and releases *Harold and Maude*, which does very poorly, both critically and commercially. (It would, however, become one of the most popular and successful cult films of all time.) Starts the production company Dumb Fuck Films with producer Chuck Mulvehill.

1972   Stephen Marshall dies of an overdose.

1973   Releases his third film, *The Last Detail*, for which for actors Jack Nicholson and Randy Quaid and screenwriter Robert Towne are Oscar nominated. Mother dies.

1975   Releases *Shampoo*, starring Warren Beatty (who is also the producer and co-writer), Julie Christie, and Goldie Hawn. The film becomes Columbia's biggest ever box office hit. Lee Grant wins a Best Supporting Actress Academy Award for her role in the movie. The film also receives nominations for Best Original Screenplay (Beatty and Robert Towne), Best Supporting Actor (Jack Warden), and Best Art Direction-Set Decoration (Richard Sylbert, W. Stewart Campbell, and George Gaines).

1976   Releases *Bound for Glory*, a biopic of Woody Guthrie starring David Carradine. The film wins Academy Awards for Best Cinematography (Haskell Wexler) and Best Adapted Score (Leonard Rosenman), and is nominated for Best Picture, Best Editing (Robert C. Jones and Pembroke J. Herring), Best Original Screenplay (Robert Getchell), and Best Costume Design (William Ware Theiss).

1978   Releases *Coming Home*, one of the first Hollywood films to address the Vietnam war, starring Jane Fonda (the originator of the project), Jon Voight, and Bruce Dern. The film wins Academy Awards for Best Actor (Voight), Best Actress (Fonda), and Best Original Screenplay (Robert C. Jones, Waldo Salt, Nancy Dowd), and is nominated for Best Picture, Best Director, Best Supporting Actor (Dern), Best Supporting Actress (Penelope Milford), and Best Editing (Don Zimmerman). Ashby shoots *Second Hand Hearts* (originally titled *Hamster of Happiness*), starring Robert Blake and Barbara Harris, the first film in three-picture deal with TV company Lorimar.

1979   Shoots and releases *Being There*, a political satire based on the book by Jerzy Kosinski, starring Peter Sellers. The film wins an Academy Award for Best Supporting Actor (Melvyn Douglas) and is nominated for Best Actor (Sellers). Ashby creates production company Northstar International with Andrew Braunsberg, the producer of *Being There*.

1980   Shoots *Lookin' To Get Out*, a gambling comedy starring Jon Voight, Burt Young, and Ann-Margret.

1981   *Second Hand Hearts* is released to terrible reviews. Dustin Hoffman asks Ashby to direct *Tootsie*, but Lorimar threatens legal action if he accepts the job. Ashby, however, is permitted to shoot *Let's Spend the Night Together*, a Rolling Stones concert film.

1982   *Lookin' To Get Out* is released after nearly two years in post-production and receives mixed reviews. Ashby's two-hour version of the film has fifteen minutes cut from it, and it is not until 2009 that his original version is finally released.

1983   *Let's Spend the Night Together* is released to modest critical and commercial success. Ashby shoots a concert movie for Neil Young's *Solo Trans* tour.

1984   Ashby shoots *The Slugger's Wife*, a romantic comedy written by Neil Simon. After a troubled production, he is fired during the editing and then reinstated with no control over the final cut.

1985   *The Slugger's Wife* is released and is a critical and commercial flop. Ashby shoots *8 Million Ways to Die*, starring Jeff Bridges and Roseanna Arquette, based on Lawrence Block's detective novel of the same name. Ashby is fired after production ends.

1986   *8 Million Ways to Die* is released to poor reviews and bad box office.

1987   Directs the pilot episode of TV show *Beverly Hills Buntz*, a spin-off of *Hill Street Blues*.

1988   Directs the pilot episode of the Graham Chapman–created TV show *Jake's Journey*. Ashby is planning to make three films (*Handcarved Coffins*, *The Hawkline Monster*, and *Vital Parts*) when he is diagnosed with pancreatic cancer. He dies on December 27, 1988.

Filmography

1970
THE LANDLORD
Cartier Productions/The Mirisch Corporation/MGM
Producer: Norman Jewison; Patrick J. Palmer (associate producer)
Director: **HAL ASHBY**
Screenplay: Bill Gunn, from the novel by Kristin Hunter
Cinematography: Gordon Willis
Production Design: Robert F. Boyle
Editing: William A. Sawyer, Edward Warschilka
Music: Al Kooper
Cast: Beau Bridges (Elgar Winthrop Julius Enders), Lee Grant (Joyce
Enders), Diana Sands (Francine "Fanny" Marie Johnson), Pearl Bailey
(Marge), Walter Brooke (William Enders Sr.), Louis Gossett Jr. (Copee
Johnson), Marki Bey (Lanie), Douglas Grant (Walter Gee Copee), **HAL
ASHBY** (cameo)
35mm, color
112 minutes

1971
HAROLD AND MAUDE
Paramount Pictures
Producer: Charles B. Mulvehill, Colin Higgins; Mildred Lewis (execu-
tive producer)
Director: **HAL ASHBY**
Screenplay: Colin Higgins
Cinematography: John Alonzo
Production Design: Michael Haller
Editing: William A. Sawyer, Edward Warschilka
Music: Cat Stevens
Cast: Ruth Gordon (Maude), Bud Cort (Harold Parker Chasen), Vivian

Pickles (Mrs. Chasen), Cyril Cusack (Glaucus), Charles Tyner (Brigadier General Victor Ball), Eric Christmas (Priest), G. Wood (Psychiatrist), **HAL ASHBY** (cameo)
35mm, color
91 minutes

1973
THE LAST DETAIL
Acrobat Productions/Bright-Persky Associates/Columbia Pictures
Producer: Lester Persky, Gerald Ayres; Charles B. Mulvehill (associate producer)
Director: **HAL ASHBY**
Screenplay: Robert Towne, from the novel by Daryl Ponicsan
Cinematography: Michael Chapman
Production Design: Michael Haller
Editing: Robert C. Jones
Music: Johnny Mandel
Cast: Jack Nicholson (Seaman's Mate First Class Billy "Bad Ass" Buddusky), Otis Young (Gunner's Mate First Class "Mule" Mulhall), Randy Quaid (Seaman Larry Meadows), Clifton James (Master at Arms), Carol Kane (Young Whore), Michael Moriarty (Marine Duty Officer), **HAL ASHBY** (cameo)
35mm, color
103 minutes

1975
SHAMPOO
Rubeeker Films/Columbia Pictures
Producer: Warren Beatty, Lester Persky; Charles H. Maguire (associate producer)
Director: **HAL ASHBY**
Screenplay: Robert Towne, Warren Beatty
Cinematography: Laszlo Kovacs
Production Design: Richard Sylbert
Editing: Robert C. Jones
Music: Paul Simon
Cast: Warren Beatty (George Roundy), Julie Christie (Jackie Shawn), Goldie Hawn (Jill), Lee Grant (Felicia Karpf), Jack Warden (Lester Karpf), Tony Bill (Johnny Pope), Carrie Fisher (Lorna Karpf), **HAL ASHBY**

(cameo, deleted)
35mm, color
109 minutes

1976
BOUND FOR GLORY
United Artists
Producer: Robert F. Blumofe, Harold Leventhal, Jeffrey M. Sneller;
Charles B. Mulvehill (associate producer)
Director: **HAL ASHBY**
Screenplay: Robert Getchell, from the book by Woody Guthrie
Cinematography: Haskell Wexler
Production Design: Michael Haller
Editing: Robert C. Jones, Pembroke J. Herring
Music: Leonard Rosenman
Cast: David Carradine (Woody Guthrie), Ronny Cox (Ozark Bule),
Melinda Dillon (Mary/Memphis Sue), Gail Strickland (Pauline), John
Lehne (Locke), Ji-Tu Cumbuka (Slim Snedeger), Randy Quaid (Luther
Johnson)
35mm, color
147 minutes

1978
COMING HOME
Jerome Hellman Productions/Jayne Productions Inc./United Artists
Producer: Jerome Hellman; Bruce Gilbert (associate producer)
Director: **HAL ASHBY**
Screenplay: Waldo Salt, Robert C. Jones; Nancy Dowd (story); Rudy
Wurlitzer (uncredited)
Cinematography: Haskell Wexler
Production Design: Michael Haller
Editing: Don Zimmerman
Cast: Jane Fonda (Sally Hyde), Jon Voight (Luke Martin), Bruce Dern
(Captain Bob Hyde), Penelope Milford (Vi Munson), Robert Carra-
dine (Bill Munson), Robert Ginty (Sergeant Dink Mobley), **HAL ASHBY**
(cameo)
35mm, color
127 minutes

1979
BEING THERE
Lorimar/Northstar International/United Artists
Producer: Andrew Braunsberg; Charles B. Mulvehill (associate producer); Jack Schwartzman (executive producer)
Director: **HAL ASHBY**
Screenplay: Jerzy Kosinski, from his own novel; Robert C. Jones (uncredited)
Cinematography: Caleb Deschanel
Production Design: Michael Haller
Editing: Don Zimmerman
Music: Johnny Mandel
Cast: Peter Sellers (Chance), Shirley MacLaine (Eve Rand), Melvyn Douglas (Benjamin Rand), Jack Warden (President "Bobby"), Richard Dysart (Dr. Robert Allenby), Richard Basehart (Vladimir Skrapinov), Ruth Attaway (Louise), **HAL ASHBY** (cameo)
35mm, color
130 minutes

1981
SECOND HAND HEARTS
Lorimar/Paramount Pictures
Producer: James William Guercio; Charles B. Mulvehill (associate producer)
Director: **HAL ASHBY**
Screenplay: Charles Eastman
Cinematography: Haskell Wexler
Production Design: Michael Haller
Editing: Amy Jones
Music: Willis Alan Ramsey
Cast: Robert Blake (Loyal Muke), Barbara Harris (Dinette Dusty), Sondra Blake (Ermy), Bert Remsen (Voyd Dusty), Shirley Stoler (Maxy), Collin Boone (Human Dusty), Amber Rose Gold (Iota)
35mm, color
102 minutes

1982
LOOKIN' TO GET OUT
Lorimar/Northstar International/Paramount Pictures

Director: **HAL ASHBY**
Producer: Robert Schaffel, Andrew Braunsberg, Edward Teets
Screenplay: Al Schwartz, Jon Voight
Cinematography: Haskell Wexler
Production Design: Robert F. Boyle
Editing: Robert C. Jones
Music: Johnny Mandel, Miles Goodman
Cast: Jon Voight (Alex Kovac), Burt Young (Jerry Feldman), Ann-Margret (Patti Warner), Bert Remsen (Smitty Carpenter), Jude Farese (Harry), Allen Keller (Joey), Richard Bradford (Bernie Gold), Stacey Pickren (Rusty), Samantha Harper (Lillian), **HAL ASHBY** (cameo)
35mm, color
105 minutes (Director's Cut: 120 mins)

1983
LET'S SPEND THE NIGHT TOGETHER
Northstar International/Raindrop/Weintraub Entertainment Group/
Embassy Pictures Corporation
Producer: Ronald L. Schwary; Kenneth J. Ryan (associate producer)
Director: Hal Ashby; Pablo Ferro (credited as "creative associate")
Cinematography: Gerald Feil, Caleb Deschanel
Editing: Lisa Day
Cast: Mick Jagger, Keith Richards, Charlie Watts, Bill Wyman, Ron Wood, **HAL ASHBY** (cameo)
35mm, color
95 minutes

1985
THE SLUGGER'S WIFE
Rastar Films/Columbia Pictures
Producer: Ray Stark; Margaret Booth (executive producer)
Director: **HAL ASHBY**
Screenplay: Neil Simon
Cinematography: Caleb Deschanel
Production Design: J. Michael Riva
Editing: Don Brochu, George C. Villaseñor; Margaret Booth (supervising editor)
Music: Patrick Williams, Quincy Jones
Cast: Michael O'Keefe (Darryl Palmer), Rebecca De Mornay (Debby

Huston Palmer), Martin Ritt (Burly DeVito), Randy Quaid (Moose
Granger), Cleavant Derricks (Manny Alvarado), Lisa Langlois (Aline
Cooper), Loudon Wainwright III (Gary), **HAL ASHBY** (cameo)
35mm, color
105 minutes

1986
8 MILLION WAYS TO DIE
PSO/TriStar Pictures
Producer: Steve Roth; Charles B. Mulvehill (coproducer); Mark Damon
(executive producer)
Director: **HAL ASHBY**
Screenplay: Oliver Stone, R. Lance Hill (as David Lee Henry), from the
novels *A Stab in the Dark* and *8 Million Ways to Die* by Lawrence Block;
Robert Towne, **HAL ASHBY**, Don Edmonds (uncredited)
Cinematography: Stephen H. Burum
Production Design: Michael Haller
Editing: Robert Lawrence, Stuart Pappé
Music: James Newton Howard
Cast: Jeff Bridges (Matt Scudder), Rosanna Arquette (Sarah), Alexandra
Paul (Sunny), Randy Brooks (Willie "Chance" Walker), Andy Garcia
(Angel Moldonado)
35mm, color
115 minutes

Hal Ashby: Interviews

Breaking Out of the Cutting Room

Hal Ashby/1970

Action 5.5 (1970). Permission to reprint provided courtesy of Directors Guild of America, Inc.

I was born in Ogden, Utah. Never a Mormon. Hated school. The last of four children. Mom and Dad divorced when I was five or six. Dad killed himself when I was twelve. I struggled toward growing up, like most others, totally confused. Joined the drop outs in my senior high year. Didn't get along with my family. Married and divorced twice before I made it to twenty-one. Hitchhiked to Los Angeles when I was seventeen. Started smoking grass at eighteen. Had about fifty or sixty jobs since I was ten, up to the time I was working as a multilith operator at good old Republic Studios.

One day, while running off ninety or so copies of some now-forgotten page fourteen, I flashed on the idea of becoming a film director. That was about fifteen years ago.

With the hope of achieving my directorial dream, I plied my multilith trade, and asked advice from those I met.

"The best school for a director is in the cutting room," was the reply I heard most often. So I looked, looked some more, and finally found a friend who would hire me as an apprentice editor. Then came the union. I applied; luckily the timing was right and I was accepted, or at least allowed to go to work.

It was good advice. When film comes into a cutting room, it holds all the work and efforts of everyone involved, up to that point. The staging, writing, acting, photography, sets, lighting, and sound. It is all there to be studied again and again and again, until you really know why it's good, or why it isn't. This doesn't tell you what is going on inside a director, or how he manages to get it from head to film, but it sure is a good way to observe the results, and the knowledge gained is invaluable.

But the life of a fledgling editor is far from ideal, and getting through it was a trip and a half. The union has an eight-year rule, which demands you work that length of time as an apprentice, or assistant, before you are eligible to edit film. It's a bad rule, which tends to debilitate those who might have any creative juices going for them at all. It can become a full-out struggle just to hang on during those eight long years, and some good talent has gone down the tubes in the process.

Desire and sheer luck were responsible for my keeping it together. First, desire made me a hard worker and kept me at it here and there for a couple of years. Then came the luck. I went to work on *The Big Country.* I was about the fourth assistant in a super large crew, headed by the chief editor, Robert Swink, but the experience was something that turned me on to film as the wildest, most exciting medium of all.

Mind-blower Number One came rushing at me the first day. One of the editors had cut his way to the end of a reel, and we all—I mean the whole crew—marched up to the projection room to look at it. Before we ran the film, somebody remembered I was the newcomer, so Bob Swink, or William Wyler, I'm not sure which, laid a little speech on me.

"If you have any ideas any no matter how wild they might seem, get them out. I, or we, might argue with you, and tell you it's a dumb idea and you are a dumb son of a bitch . . . but that doesn't matter because the heat of our anger comes only from the desire to make a good film. You must understand how we all *feel* about this film, or any film, and know in your heart that the words said in anger have nothing to do with anything personal. It will sound that way because we are driven by those strong feelings, and we don't take the time to be polite, but personal it isn't. So get those ideas out into the open and remember, the only thing any of us wants out of all this is to make a good film."

Needless to say; there was a lot of yelling, hollering, and swearing that went on down in those cutting rooms, but there were also about eighteen tons of love floating around there, too.

It was, indeed, a beautiful year!

Some more good time was spent . . . Bob Swink took me with him from film to film. *The Diary of Anne Frank, The Young Doctors, The Children's Hour, The Best Man,* and a couple of others.

When I was lucky enough to be working with Bob, he hit me with everything from the technical aspects to a philosophy of film.

"Once the film is in hand," he would say, "forget about the script, throw away all of the so-called rules, and don't try to second-guess the director. Just look at the film, and let it guide you. It will turn you on all by itself, and you'll have more ideas on ways to cut it than you would ever dream possible.

"And use your instincts! Don't be afraid of them! Rely on them! After all, with the exception of a little knowledge, instincts are all we've got.

"Also, don't be afraid of the film. You can cut it together twenty-six different ways, and if none of those works, you can always put it back into daily form, and start over."

As I watched and absorbed, Bob proved editing to be a truly creative force, and it really turned me around. I almost, but not quite, forgot about wanting to be a director.

Finally, my eight years were up. Bob got me on *The Greatest Story Ever Told* as a fourth editor. After a few months I left, and went over to *The Loved One* as chief editor. The George Stevens people were mad at me—I hope they still aren't.

I did the first cut on *The Loved One*, but that was it. Tony Richardson had a commitment in London, so he took the film with him to finish it there, and left me here. It was a bad time. Depression and paranoia ran rampant. In short, I was on the super bummer of the year.

Then some more good luck came my way, via John Calley, who produced *The Loved One*. John knew Norman Jewison was looking for an editor, so he set up an introduction. It must have been a good meeting, because Norman took a chance, and I ended up cutting *The Cincinnati Kid*. I also got my head together at the same time. I was feelin' good, and from there on, things really happened.

I worked with Norman on *The Russians Are Coming, The Russians Are Coming, In the Heat of the Night*, and *The Thomas Crown Affair*. It was the most productive relationship imaginable. From in front, Norman always gave me good film. Then, to top it off, he trusted me and my instincts. He never stood behind me in the cutting room. He let me select and cut his film as I felt it. It was an editor's dream and, in the end, it brought me two Academy nominations, and one Oscar.

As time marched on, Norman boosted me up to the position of associate producer, and I was able to gain some of the much needed experience in the areas of pre-production and production. Norman had me involved in everything from scouting locations to being used as a sounding board for ideas on script, casting, and new projects. It was the total trip, and I really felt as if I were giving as much to the film as possible, without actually being the director. What more could I ask?

What's really wild is the fact that I didn't even have to ask!

One day, while we were working on *Thomas Crown*, Norman looked at me, smiled, then asked: "What do you want to do?" It really blew my mind. In all the time I had known Norman, we never once touched upon the subject, and here this beautiful, sensitive dude was standing there asking me about my dream.

"Well, I want to make films," I said. Christ, I couldn't even get the damn word out of my mouth.

Another long moment while Norman just stood there with his impish grin. Finally, it came out.

"I want to direct. That's where it's at, isn't it?" I said.

"Right!" Norman replied. "So let's find something for you." And he did!

Of course, it didn't happen just like that, but happen it did. We were still shooting *Gaily, Gaily*, when Bill Gunn sent the first eighty-two pages of his first draft on *The Landlord*. Norman and I read it, and were both very up on Bill's screenplay and anxious to receive the forty, or so, pages still due. Then, in the simplest manner possible, Norman said, "Why don't you direct *Landlord*?" I jumped up and did a fast dance around the office.

Landlord was initially set as a project for Norman, but he had a couple of time schedule problems still unsolved, so he laid it on me.

I immediately took the pages we had to my dear and close friend, Beau Bridges. Beau read the pages and said yes. I was home free. One whole day as a director. One major decision made. And no rejections.

In the meantime, Norman had set things in motion to gain approval from the brothers Mirisch, and United Artists. Not an easy task, I'm sure, to ask for two million dollars so some unknown factor of a director can make his first film. Nobody ever made mention of it to me—at least I don't recollect having ever talked about it to Norman—but it certainly crossed my mind, as it must have crossed some others. They probably even talked of it in some circles. *It* being what I call deductive knowledge.

Mainly: "If Ashby falls on his ass, Jewison can take over and we'll be covered."

I honestly don't know if anyone ever had such a thought, but I do know Norman was my producer, and for that I am truly thankful.

So I had the financing, a script, a star, a producer, me, and the absolute need to fulfill about 1080 un-made decisions. All of them to be resolved before the first day of shooting. And once you get there, as I later discovered, the pace jumps up to about 1080 fast decisions per day.

I was really learning the difference between being a sounding board and using a sounding board. I couldn't just sit around the office and rap with Norman about the script, or the casting, anymore. Now I found myself with the responsibility of making decisions. Final decisions. It was nervous time.

We were into the casting, and I really do believe it was the toughest time on the film. Maybe that was so because it was the first time I had been forced to make such a definite commitment. Not words on paper. Or film to be cut, then changed later.

This time, when the decision was made, that was it. Not to be changed. Of course, as I look back, I'm sure the major fear I had about my being a director was taking its toll. The fear of not being able to communicate my thoughts to the actors.

I felt fairly secure in all other areas, such as the visual aspects, and I never doubted for a moment the abilities of the actors I chose to play the parts. No, the knowledge I had gained as an editor would serve its purpose well, but it had nothing to do with telling an actor what I wanted.

Beau was a friend, so the fear subsided somewhat when it came to him, but how was it going to go with Lee Grant, Diana Sands, Lou Gossett, or Pearl Bailey? I had no way of knowing. Time, as they say, would tell—but that didn't help at all. By that time, it could be too late.

The snowball was rolling, and some super good people were around to help it grow. As production manager, Pat Palmer was the greatest. But his talents went much, much beyond that, and he took on the chores of associate producer, too. The gigantic talents of Bob Boyle were being used to do the best damn job ever as the production designer and art director. I didn't know Terry Nelson, who was going to be my first assistant director, but my instincts said, "Yes!" the moment we met. As time went on, they were proved right.

The time had indeed come! This was it! We had a week or so of rehearsals in New York, and everybody got to know each other. I had hopes this would ease some of the fears I held about the communication with actors thing, but it seems luck was definitely not with me.

The first day of directing my first film, and I couldn't breathe. The damn fear had actually managed to make me sick. The doctor came to the location, checked me over, and said I had walking pneumonia. I would have to go to bed. I said, "Hell, no!" and told him to pump everything he had into my arm, rear, or foot, if necessary. He did just that and, three days later, I was a well man with three days of directing my first film forever behind me.

Within a week, I had completely rid myself of that old communication fear, and we were on our way. Norman, as usual, was doing everything right. To stress his point that it was my film, he stayed away from New York. He didn't want to run the risk of intimidating me by standing around in the background, getting nervous, and maybe suggesting a shot now and then.

Pressures there were. The first thing the Mirisch Company came down on was the photography. It was too dark. They couldn't see the actor's eyes. I explained how I wanted the look of the ghetto footage to have the etched feeling it did so we would have a contrast to the so-called, blown out, billowy, white-on-white sequences which we would be shooting in a few weeks.

"But this is a comedy," Walter Mirisch said, "and you've just got to see their eyes."

Then I would get into how I could see their eyes, and how nice it would be if they would just have a little faith in me, and trust me. It went on and on, with neither side giving in, until we got to the so-called white footage. Then I guess they saw what I meant, and the pressure of that issue eased off.

But there were other things to get them up-tight, too. I had fallen behind schedule and, on top of that, I was shooting a tremendous amount of film, much more than normal. As to the schedule, what the hell could I say? I wasn't any happier about it than they were.

We did run into fourteen days of rain while shooting out on Long Island, but the main reason for being behind was me. I set the pace, and that was that. Actually, it wasn't a slow pace at all. We were running our tails off, and the idea of being behind really ate away at me.

After we were six weeks into the shooting, Pat Palmer rescheduled the picture. He wanted to ease my anxiety, and enough time had elapsed for him to study and gauge my tempo so he could come up with a more realistic schedule to fit me.

As usual, Pat hit it right on the nose. Then we were right on, and I, for one, felt much, much better. I'm not sure if the complaints were fewer, or if I just ignored them, but I didn't notice them as much.

And then it was over. It took sixty-six days and two million, four hundred thousand dollars—about four hundred thousand over budget—to do it, but we did it, and the shooting was finished.

A goodly portion of the overage was spent on post-production. I really did shoot a lot of film. A lot more than I realized. In one sense, it was okay; I believe the more film you have, the more latitude you have, but I was floored when I saw what a load I had placed on Bill Sawyer, the editor.

Bill had been in L.A. during the shooting, and I, the ex editor, didn't have any idea of just how much film we had. To help Bill out, I jumped in and took a couple of sequences to cut, and we put another editor, Ed Warschilka, to work as well.

Did I encounter any surprises?

Yes, one very pleasant and nice surprise. I believe one of the best things a director can do for his film is to get as many others as possible to become a part of the film. Get their creative juices turned on, and most people will give and give and give. To gain this end, I submerged my ego so it wouldn't be out there getting in the way of someone else who might be able to get it on, given half a chance, and really contribute something special.

As I honestly practiced such a policy, it really blew my mind when I sat there looking at the dailies and saw so much of me coming out on that screen. For some reason, I hadn't expected any such thing, but I must say my ego was most pleased to see it happen. It was indeed a most wonderful surprise.

Will I do anything different next time?

Yes, I will try to apply even more concentration. I had a tendency to try and get away from the film for a few hours each evening, hoping for a fresher outlook the next day. I don't think that is where it's at any more, so I will try, on the next one, to give it twenty-four hours of concentration each day, during the entire shooting.

Students often ask me how they can become directors. The only thing I can tell them is this: "Don't follow my example. The cutting room is an excellent place to learn much about directing, but that eight-year rule is ridiculous.

"So forget that whole scene, and go out and make a film. Any kind of film. Do a short ten- or twenty-minute film on a shoestring, or borrow forty thousand dollars and make a feature. If it's good, it will be seen.

"Above all else, put as much honesty as you can into everything. That's what comes across on the screen: Honesty."

Director Hal Ashby's Office Is a House with Psychedelic Walls

Steve Toy/1971

From *Variety*, December 24, 1972. Used with permission of Variety. Copyright © 2009 Reed Business Information, a division of Reed Elsevier, Inc. All rights reserved.

The Oscar stands in the middle of it all.

The walls are painted psychedelic; the rugs, of assorted shapes and sizes, are strewn without format throughout.

An enormous couch with pillows occupies the center of the room not far from a crackling fireplace.

"This is a real trip," said Hal Ashby about his home that could have been designed by Alice B. Toklas. "Paramount asked me where I wanted my offices. I told them I've always wanted a house."

And he got it—one appropriate for the director whose granddaddy beard stretches haphazardly down his chest and hair touches his shoulders.

An Academy winner for editing of *In the Heat of the Night*, he directed *The Landlord* and the current *Harold and Maude*.

Yet there are no traces of him ever occupying a chair with his name on the back.

"This costs less than the space at Goldwyn," Ashby said.

It Really Works

"We did all of the pre-production and editing for *Harold and Maude* here. It really works well. When we got into casting, it set the people more at ease."

An enormous complex of editing equipment that occupies a wall of the dining room clashes with the large crystal chandelier.

"I don't know of any other directors operating like this. Most work out of a studio. This is far-out."

Underneath the hair is a forty-two-year-old man who started in the industry as a multilith machine operator, worked for eight years from apprentice editor up, before beginning to direct.

He's part of a new breed that shuns Hollywood society—his idea of a party is six or seven people rapping in his living room—and all that goes with it.

"This definitely gets comment from everybody—Paramount likes it. We had a meeting up here with Columbia officials. If some of them didn't like it, they didn't vocalize it."

A haze covers the city seen from his window high in the Hollywood Hills.

It's the most elaborate place he's ever lived.

"Many years ago in Van Nuys I was out of work. I went to the state employment office. I waited an hour to see the interviewer. I saw this lady and told her I wanted to get into the motion picture business. She looked at me like I was crazy. Then she said she had something for a multilith operator.

"I started meeting people, and I got a direction of where I wanted to go. I knew it was directing. I asked people what to do. They told me to go into editorial."

Totally Turned On

"I really did want to tell stories on film. And directing is the most fulfilled way of getting my interpretation of my idea on the screen. Once I got into it I was totally turned on by it."

He lights a miniature cigaret.

His hair, he said, "is a symbol of where certain people's heads are."

His Basic Philosophy

"There are so many euphemisms. 'Hippie' encompasses more people. The basic philosophy of wanting to further peace or love—I'm very much in favor of that. How to attain it is another question.

"And I believe human values are more important than material values. I've never had a thing on material things. This is all rented. It's the best place I ever lived. I lived at the studio in a bungalow for two years."

Two black cats stroll by.

The social aspects of Hollywood, he said, will break down as the financial system has.

He walks into the dining room to show off the equipment.

"I'm down here at 3 a.m. sometimes—you couldn't do that if all this were at a studio."

He laughs and takes a sip of Sanka.

He walks back to his chair—colorful, with the usual pillows—and rests.

He never once looked at Oscar.

Director Charges Studio Was Afraid of *Maude*

Marilyn Beck/1972

From *The Evening Bulletin.* January 25, 1972. By permission of Marilyn Beck and Creators Syndicate, Inc.

HOLLYWOOD—*Harold and Maude* director Hal Ashby admits he's mighty disappointed at the weak audience response to his black comedy.

He's convinced there would be many more coins jingling into theater box offices if Paramount had done a better job of promoting the Ruth Gordon–Bud Cort starrer.

"Paramount has gone out of its way," says the soft-spoken filmmaker, "to see that there's been no mention in ads of the fact this is a love affair between an eighty-year-old woman and a young boy."

They've run scared, Ashby feels, and "approached the subject so that it leads people to suspect this is a simple, nice relationship between two nice people."

To prove his point, he points out that in Baltimore the film's distributor used his own hard-hitting ad campaign, "promoting the film like it is. And we ended up with our best box-office in that city."

Ashby is not the sort to become riled by such sort of studio maneuvering, but, as he explains, "When you've devoted a year-and-a-half to something, you watch and fret over it as you would a child."

He recalls the joy of filming the picture in and around the San Francisco area, maintaining that, until this period of after-the-fact aggravation, everything about the project went swimmingly.

"There were some moments of uncertainty," he admits, "when we set about shooting in the exclusive area of Hillsboro. The last time a film company was there was for an Otto Preminger project and I understand he went through that community like a storm trooper, leaving residents with strong feelings that they'd just as soon prefer film companies didn't invade their borders again. But we weren't given one bit of trouble. Everything went fine."

The Hillsboro home that the *Harold and Maude* company rented for their mansion scenes is currently on the market for $500,000 unfurnished, $7 million furnished.

"You can imagine working in those kind of surroundings," says Ashby. "Rare antiques, two hangings worth a million each. I didn't even dare smoke a cigaret for fear I'd burn something."

Hal Ashby

Robert David Crane and Christopher Fryer/1972

From *Jack Nicholson Face to Face*. M. Evans & Co. 1975. 100–16. Reprinted with permission of Rowman & Littlefield Publishing Group.

Looking at gray-bearded Hal Ashby sitting cross-legged on top of his bed on the second floor of his home high atop Laurel Canyon suggests a misplaced guru.

Ashby is, in fact, a film editor turned director. He had a long and successful association with Norman Jewison as a film editor, culminating in winning the Academy Award in 1967 for editing *In the Heat of the Night*. In 1969 Jewison produced Ashby's directorial debut, *The Landlord*, which was critically acclaimed but did only fair business at the box office. In 1971 his second film, *Harold and Maude*, was released to a totally lesser reaction than his debut film.

In the summer of 1972 he was to begin his third film, starring Jack Nicholson for MGM, but after many unresolved differences over script and casting the project was canceled. Nicholson and Ashby wanted to work together, though, and in November of the same year they were to leave for Toronto to begin shooting the Robert Towne screenplay, *The Last Detail*.

Ashby followed the enormously successful *The Last Detail* with *Shampoo*, the story of a Beverly Hills hairdresser and his many adventures, starring Warren Beatty, Julie Christie, and Goldie Hawn, and written by Robert Towne and Warren Beatty.

In the summer of 1974 there was a re-release of *Harold and Maude* for a limited engagement because Paramount realized that there was a growing cult for the film and the work of a major new director, Hal Ashby.

As we began to get ready for the interview, attended by Chuck Mulvehill (Ashby's assistant) and an unidentified woman, we quickly noticed that Ashby is an art lover. The house was sparsely furnished, but in a rich manner specifically suggesting his love for rock music, for example, a colorful painting montage of the Rolling Stones and Neil Young.

As Mulvehill tried to wake Ashby up with some coffee, we settled in our director-style chairs and were informed that Ashby, Nicholson, cast, and crew would be leaving the following week for Toronto to start production.

Question: How did you first come into contact with Jack?

Hal Ashby: My first contact with him came when I was doing *Harold and Maude*, and I was at Bob Evans's house discussing the film with Bob, and Jack happened to be visiting there, and he took the time to come over and introduce himself, and sit down, and tell me how he enjoyed my first film, *The Landlord*, and a few things about it. So the first contact I had with him was purely on a social level like that.

Then I was involved in a film over at MGM that I thought Jack would be right for, so I made contact with him, and I took the script up to him, and I sat with him, and sat with him a number of times from the first time on, and about six weeks after that he said he would do the project. But everything ended up in a mess over at MGM, and we didn't do it.

Question: What caused the cancellation of the film?

Ashby: What happened to it was, I was going to do this film, and I finally got it down to where Jack agreed to do it—it was called *Three-Cornered Circle*, and it was taken from *The Postman Always Rings Twice*—and at that point I wanted to cast Michelle Phillips in the girl's role, and another actor in the other role, and it just came to a gigantic dispute with MGM as to how to cast my film. I guess they'd say their film; I say my film. I just couldn't work that way; I'm sure there are some people that can let the studios cast their films. It wasn't the kind of film-making that I was used to, or could actually get involved in. It became very messy at that stage, and I had to say no, and then they said no, and then Jack, in essence, said no, too. I would assume that his reasons for saying no were basically the same as mine. What their ideas on the casting were I really don't one hundred percent know. It just wasn't the way that I saw it. I'd been involved with it for about three months, but if it had been laid out in front exactly what they wanted I never would have been involved in it in the first place. For myself, I was under the impression that they (MGM) wanted to attract film-makers over there, because they had quite a bad reputation. They got Danny Melnick in, and maybe someday he'll make that thing work, but what they want to do now is to attract guys and still give them the old "yes" and "no." That results in a breakdown in communication. Whenever you have somebody coming in and saying, "You have to do this," or "You have to do that," then something, somewhere, is going to get up tight. In this case it was me.

Question: So MGM owns the project, then?

Ashby: Oh, yes, they've always owned it, because they made the film of *The Postman Always Rings Twice*. Gordon Carroll was going to produce it for them, and he had talked to me about the script, and I read it and I saw some good possibilities in it. I made my deal, and from that point on went after Jack. I was really happy when I got him. I thought it was a big, big plus. I wanted to use Michelle. First of all, on one level she's a much bigger name than they think she is, because those people don't know anything about the music business. They really don't. I mean, besides Michelle, you could mention someone like Leon Russell, and they'd say, "Isn't he some country-folk singer or something?" Or you say Neil Young, and they say, "I don't know him." That's kind of a weird experience in its own right, in that they wouldn't keep up on all the levels of the entertainment business especially on the level that they basically function at, which is a financial level. You'd think they'd look around and see who's making a lot of money, if they just want to go at it at that level.

Also, because of the relationship between Jack and Michelle, I thought that they would be very exciting together on film. I really thought Michelle had it. I was almost locked into Michelle before we got Jack, as a matter of fact.

Question: Why did it take so long to get Jack?

Ashby: I think just because he's very, very thoughtful about what he does do. That was basically what it was. You know, he's had a lot of things come to him, obviously. And he has a lot of things to consider, you know, like how does that role compare to the last one, and to the next one that he thinks he might be doing.

As for myself, I can't remember picking up a script and deciding on it in less time than he did.

Question: What did you think of *The King of Marvin Gardens*?

Ashby: I liked it. I understand there's been a lot of negativism about it, and so forth, but I was pleased for Jack, and I was pleased for Rafelson because I thought they did a remarkable job. Jack's character was certainly different from anything he's ever done before. He sold me; I believed that character. I thought Bruce Dern was marvelous. And certainly, Ellen Burstyn was great. I haven't read any reviews for it, except for a little mention it got in an article about the New York Film Festival in *Newsweek*, but I don't really know what the reviewers are taking out after. I'm not really sure where their heads are, but then I never am, in that sense. I thought it was a very daring thing, because it was out of the mainstream of films, or where they want you to go with films, or what characters they want you to have on the screen. That's why I found it intriguing. I liked the look of the film, the locale where they put it, those two interesting brothers, and making Jack the introverted of the two brothers, which was not the usual casting. I thought he was marvelous.

Question: Can you tell us how all the elements came together in *The Last Detail*?

Ashby: I became involved in it out of the MGM deal; Jack was already involved in it, and they were just at the stage when they were beginning to look for a director. Jack was in it, Gerry Ayres was producing it. We had talked a little bit about it before, but not very much, when we were doing the MGM thing, but I figured it wouldn't happen for me, because since this had to be done in the winter, I'd probably still be in post-production on the MGM thing. Well, when the MGM thing fell apart Jack said, "Why don't we try and move you over and get you to do this?" And I said, "That would be great." It got a little bit messy for awhile, because I was involved in a thing over at Warner Brothers at the same time, but I really wanted to do *Last Detail*.

Question: Can you tell us a little bit about the story?

Ashby: Yeah, I really like the story. It deals with three sailors, but two of them are lifers, one of which is Jack. And Jack and the other sailor, who's black, are in transit, like at Norfolk, and Jack's been in twelve years, and the other guy, Mule, has been in fourteen years—they don't know each other. They're in separate transient barracks, just awaiting orders, and they pull this temporary detail as chasers, as SPs, to take this eighteen year-old kid up to Portsmouth, New Hampshire. He's rather naive, naive because of a lack of life experiences, and he's a kleptomaniac who just stole money from the wrong fund. It was the commanding officer's favorite charity, and they really gave him a rather hard sentence.

As for the two lifers, they're just going to get him up there and come back on kind of a paid liberty. They first go by bus to Richmond, and then they take the train, and the relationship starts to build between these three guys. It becomes episodic, with all the things they fall into and get involved in. It also deals a lot with people doing their jobs and how that fucks everybody up. Of course, when you get two guys like this in situations there's a lot of good humor in it. But on the other level it's a good character study. You've got a couple of lifers that are very complicated characters. It's interesting to see what motivates them and helps them get through life. They've got their own things going; they couldn't give a shit about this dumb kid when it starts, they're kind of parental towards him; they still don't know how to break out of that other mold. What we'd like them to do is for all of them to go to Canada and blow the whole thing off, but I don't think that would be honest either. We go through that all the time, showing what they are, rather than what we'd like them to do. So by the time we get to the point where the kid, who's not really dumb, but he's not really bright either, decides that he really wants to get away, he can't because he's concerned about what will happen to these two guys. He doesn't want to get away, because he knows it will be their ass. At the same time, they'd like to see him get away, but they know they can't let him. So there's a lot of complexities involved, which I think will be very, very good. I'm very high on it. Bob Towne did the screenplay, who's a longtime writer, and a very particular writer who doesn't put his name on a lot of things. He's a long-time friend of Jack's.

Question: How is Jack preparing for this role?

Ashby: The way I see it, Jack prepares for a role as well as an actor can. He tries to look at as many different thoughts or sides that the character might have at any given time, and constantly questioning that, especially at this stage. I spent yesterday with him, and I'm going to spend today with him again, just really going through the script and questioning things. That doesn't really mean that we're solidifying the answers right now, but what we're doing is narrowing it down from twenty possibilities to five possibilities in hopes of getting to the one possibility for this complex character that we both want.

Question: Do you believe in rehearsing with the cast as a group, or do you like to work just on a one-to-one basis?

Ashby: On this one, since it's basically a three-character story, I won't really rehearse with the people that they run into along the way. We'll basically do read-through rehearsals about a week before, so we can all talk about each other's characters and so forth. If we can get the relationship of the characters established in the read-throughs, then I think the spontaneity will happen on its own, which is important to a film. We're going to try and shoot as much in continuity, at least the heavy scenes, as we can. Usually continuity doesn't matter; it's all part of film-making, and sometimes it's interesting, it's part of the game, but in this, since it is a character study, I wanted to do it in continuity, especially in respect of the unfolding of the relationship with the boy.

Question: Do you have the actors set for the other two parts?

Ashby: The other sailor isn't set yet. We were going to do it with Rupert Crosse, but there have been some problems which we're still trying to work out, in fact, desperately trying to work out, because we're getting so close. Rupert would have been marvelous. We've set the boy. A boy by the name of Randy Quaid. He's the kid from *The Last Picture Show* who took Cybill Shepherd to the swimming party; kind of a strange looking kid. He's big, too. I like him; I like his quality. I had a feeling we'd have a good start with him, because he has kind of a naive quality. He doesn't look like he's off the streets of New York. And visually, I think his size is going to work for us. He's not the classic small guy who's always getting picked on.

Question: What makes this film different for you from *The Landlord* and *Harold and Maude*?

Ashby: I think it's the subject matter more than anything else. In essence, it deals with the military and military justice, and what a lot of shit all that is, but it doesn't profess to give any answers, but it lays a lot of it out, and that's something that's always intrigued me. Intrigued me in the sense that the story's worth being told in all those areas, and I liked this one because it doesn't go after the obvious. We're not saying that he did something wrong in Vietnam that he's being called on the floor for, but he did something wrong here, and it's still military justice in the way that they respond. It deals with guys who are lifers in the service, and how they respond. It's about bondage—this is all on an intellectual level, of course, we never get into dialogues about it, but it's stuff that we fight for to come out.

Question: What qualities do you think Jack has that attracts filmgoers to his movies?

Ashby: Film is a very personal medium, at least for me it is. I think basically there's an honesty to Jack that comes through. But then again, it's on an ethereal level. People aren't watching the film and saying, "Gee, I like his honesty, and that's why I like to see his films." That's just not the way it happens; people feel a kind of electricity, an attraction to this person to watch him and see what he does, because you're never exactly sure what he is going to do, and I think that's the kind of thing that's fascinating. Like in *Marvin Gardens*, even though Jack is playing a subdued character, it's interesting because it's not what I expected him to do. I'm not four reels ahead of him, saying "This is gonna happen, this is gonna happen, this is gonna happen." An actor in film has to have a real sense of honesty, whereas some actors put up a façade, and you don't feel that you ever get through to them. With Jack there is no façade; it's just right out there. There is just innately a great appeal to a lot of people for that sort of thing. I may be intellectualizing it, but I think that's what a lot of the draw is. We all know that he did quite a few pictures before *Easy Rider*, but when he came on the screen in *Easy Rider*, you went, "Wow, here comes somebody, let's watch this." And it's a great thing because it isn't forced, he isn't pushing like hell to make it happen. Whether he's pushing like hell inside to make the character happen doesn't matter, because again if he is doing it, he's doing it very honestly and you're not put off by it. That's one of the differences between Jack and Steve McQueen. Steve is much more of a personality actor, and he tends to be less honest. Jack's honesty is his great attraction to the people because they feel like they really know him.

Jack is really a special guy; on all levels, too. I loved his picture, *Drive*, that he directed, and he's written some great things. I thought *Ride in the Whirlwind* was a hell of a picture. He's done a lot of different things on really deep levels.

Question: Can you characterize Jack Nicholson in one sentence?

Ashby: To put it down in the simplest terms I think Jack is just great—a great person and a great talent, and I love him.

Shampoo: Film & Filmmaker

A. Leigh Charlton/1975

From UCLA *Daily Bruin*, March 3, 1975.

Shampoo and its director Hal Ashby are very much alike—their unpretentious exterior camouflages an inner profundity. For all its big name star power (Warren Beatty, Julie Christie, Goldie Hawn, screenplay by Robert Towne, photography by Laszlo Kovacs), *Shampoo* is still a film with depth and subtlety. And for all his recent success as a director (this is his fourth film, preceded by *The Last Detail, Harold and Maude*, and *The Landlord*), Ashby has retained the low profile image more in keeping with his years spent in the editing room than his current position behind the camera.

Ashby, Beatty, and Towne sat down together in November of '73 to cull one screenplay out of two (Beatty and Towne each had written their own script). By March of '74 a powerhouse cast had been assembled, including Jack Warden, Lee Grant, and Tony Bill as well as the big three, and shooting began. By the end of May, Wycherly's seventeenth-century play, *The Country Wife*, the tale of a Don Juan in eunuch's clothing, had become two days in the life of a Beverly Hills hairdresser.

It is no accident that the story is centered around Election Day, 1968. In this comedy of musical beds, there is an undercurrent of political irony that continually puts the antics of George, Jill, Jackie, Felicia, and Lester in perspective. When Lester bemusedly notes the temporariness of life in general and love in particular, he is standing in front of a television ignorant of Nixon's simultaneous pledge to bind up the country's wounds and "bring us back together again."

This multi-leveled reality is a subtle dimension that adds immeasurably to the overall impact of the film. It is one of the factors that

23

will enable it to endure, and probably improve with age, not only as delightful entertainment, but as an astute time capsule.

In the words of its director, "There's nothing wrong with entertainment, if it's good entertainment. Usually pure entertainment has other things underneath it. I've never looked at *Shampoo* just as pure entertainment; hopefully if it's a good film, it will be entertaining."

Indicating his own political awareness he added, "When Nixon was elected in '68 it meant more than many people realized at the time. There was a gigantic change during that election. In the film we've got a lot of people running around talking about it, some of them ignore it; no one goes and votes. There's a party with big contributors and one where no one is paying attention to anything." Important as that point in time is to the film and the filmmakers, it remains the backdrop against which the characters play out their comic drama, one layer of a rich confection.

Warren Beatty is irresistible as the man who loves continually, but not wisely. No other actor could possibly capture the magnetism and vulnerability that Beatty personifies so naturally. Dressed seductively in radical chic, packing his hair blower like a pistol, he is the epitome of physical perfection; more an object to be worshiped than a human being who can feel pain. The package is even more attractive because George (Beatty) doesn't wield his attractiveness as a weapon; in fact, he seems almost unaware of his uncommon beauty.

As his current girlfriend Jill, Goldie Hawn is as gorgeous as she is talented. This is the first role that has tapped the mature woman that lies beneath the baby-doll blonde hair and innocent eyes. Her bubbly energy is contained and the result is a performance that confirms the adage that less is more.

Julie Christie is a sympathetic queen bitch and how she manages to be both simultaneously is a secret that only she can reveal. With her straight hair, bangs, and miniskirts, Christie is the quintessential late sixties beauty. Not only are she and Beatty the screen's most attractive couple, but in her pouting, sensual way she is the only actress who can mouth obscenities and still be beautiful.

Lee Grant accepts the challenge of Felicia, a callous, spoiled Beverly Hills matron (who is as obnoxious in bed as she is around the dinner table) with relish, and manages to create a fresh interpretation out of an overworked stereotype. A skillful bit of writing makes the least likeable character the biggest loser in the end and she brings Felicia through all the changes gracefully. For those who have seen *The Landlord*, the excellence of her work under Ashby comes as no surprise.

The surprise performance comes from Jack Warden, last seen as the title character's coarse, cab-driving father in *Duddy Kravitz*. As Lester, the big-wig financial advisor who keeps his mistress (Jackie) in luxurious seclusion to protect his image, he represents conventional, acceptable amorality. Revealing himself to be a skillful comedian, Warden seems to know Lester so well that the term acting simply doesn't apply. When he and George face off over Jackie (and Felicia and Lorna and . . .), Lester realizes that George is more the fool than the fox, and accepts him for what he is—king of the king-sized, but unable to get it together in the real world.

To Ashby's credit, these broad characters never fall into caricatures and although the action proceeds at breakneck speed, it never seems forced or illogical.

These "pop" characters represent a change for the director from the off-beat and the out-casts he has worked with previously. Nevertheless, Ashby maintains that *Shampoo* is as close to him as any of his other films that might seem to be more personal. "It's just different characters in a different situation," he says. "The overall philosophy of every filmmaker, what he basically feels, will come through in his films, no matter what characters he's dealing with. Your basic values, what you think a human being's rights are, will be there. It just happens, I don't know how. When I first saw it in *The Landlord*, I was surprised." When asked to articulate his "personal philosophy," however, Ashby declined, saying "I've never sat down and thought to put this, this, and this in my films."

Ashby would elaborate on his feelings about the characters: "They're caught up in a particular situation at a particular time in their lives. They're not living their lives in the way I would consider ideal so consequently our concern was not to be too harsh on them. At the same time, I'm not going to be the one to sort it all out because that doesn't happen, either. Someone isn't there to say, 'Gee, if you'd do this or do that things might be a little bit better or you might get a little bit more of what you want, or think you want.'"

In *Shampoo* it's the small moments, the subtle details in the characters, the clothes, the dialogue, the atmosphere, that make it work. Actually, the characters are more routine than extraordinary; but that is a large part of their charm. Ashby is one director who is at home exploring the subtleties of his characters: "Since *Shampoo* covers such a short period of time you don't go for a large scope, saying this person is going to start over here and end up over there and change in this particular way. There's not a lot of changes that go in the characters, at least not visible, surface changes. Hopefully there are emotional things pulling at each and every one of them. That's what I really wanted to show—what happens to emotions in different ways."

When asked about the possibility of such characterizations being interpreted as superficial, Ashby answered, "We certainly never though of it as superficial. We wanted to get down as much as possible, but in that short period of time we knew there wouldn't be great character changes. We're not trying to say it isn't (superficial) either. We're not trying to get in great messages by articulating them in dialogue. We've had a lot of fun with some of the characters, but we also want to show there's a bit of pain. To me that takes away from superficiality."

Ashby laughingly described the function of a director as the one who "sees that it all gets done." This is no small understatement given the dynamics of working on film, much less one that is produced and co-written by its star (Beatty). In referring to his work on the film, Ashby uses the plural "we" rather than the singular "I" and it is apparent that this is a genuine emotional, as well as professional, distinction. Refreshingly unegotistical, Ashby speaks of film as a totally collaborative medium. "It takes all kinds of people, everybody working hard." He considers it stimulating rather than threatening to work with creative people: "There's a chance to get more periphery, more subtlety going on because of the number of people you bring into it. One thing I'd always want to stay away from, no matter if I were to write, produce, and direct, would be to become too rigid and say, 'Let's do it exactly this way.' That doesn't mean it can't be that way. There are directors that work that way and they do marvelous work, but it's always scared me a little bit." Admitting that his next film, however, will be billed as "A Hal Ashby Film," he adds, "I'm not sure what that means exactly."

In the spirit of a true collaborator, Ashby acknowledged Towne's fine script and discussed his handling of it: "We stayed very close to the script because it was very full. There's a lot of dialogue so there wasn't really much room for improvisation out and beyond that. We would concentrate on tightening each scene during shooting as much as we could." As for photographer Kovacs, who captures L.A. and all its deca-

dent lushness so beautifully: "When I'm shooting, the person I'm closest with on the set is the cameraman. He's my eyes."

Although older chronologically than many of the up and coming
filmmakers included in *Esquire* magazine's Ninth Wave, Hal Ashby, by
virtue of his attitude, is more youthful than many of his colleagues
who cull their ideas from late night movies. In his quiet way he manages to infuse everything he does with unequaled credibility (in *Shampoo*
he creates the definitive sixties psychedelic party, complete with *Sergeant Pepper* and Jimi Hendrix). When we spoke he was already deeply
immersed in his next project, Woody Guthrie's autobiography, *Bound
for Glory*. The screenplay, written by Robert Getchell (*Alice Doesn't Live
Here Anymore*), had been shown to him and the attraction was as immediate as it was natural. As it's planned now, the film will concentrate
on a formative four-year period in Woody's young life (from '36–'39)
when he was on the road looking for himself. With the combination
of fascinating characters, honest humor, politics (Woody was part of
the Oakie migration to California), music, and pain this project seems
tailor-made for Hal Ashby, a man who is content to walk softly.

Film Guru Ashby Enjoys View from the Mountain

Will Jones/1976

From the *Minneapolis Star Tribune*, February 8, 1976. Reprinted with permission of *Star Tribune*.

The closest I've come to climbing a mountain to visit a wise man was a drive up into Laurel Canyon the other day to an area called Lookout Mountain to pay a call on Hal Ashby.

There, in a house with a splendid view of Los Angeles and Hollywood in one direction and the San Fernando Valley in another, is where the man who directed *Harold and Maude* and *The Last Detail*, and *Shampoo* puts together his movies.

Ashby, barefooted, bearded, and T-shirted and radiating serenity, is as good a candidate for guruhood as any. And a mountaintop is certainly a fitting place for a visitor from Minneapolis to find the man who made *Harold and Maude*, the film that seems destined to run more or less forever in one Twin Cities theater or another. Ms. Jones, who never has displayed any overt foot fetishism in the past, admitted later that she repressed a strong urge to sit at Ashby's feet, not necessarily as homage in behalf of our area's *Harold and Maude* cult, but simply because the man has graceful, beautiful feet.

Ashby used to live in the house, and rented a house next door to use as an office and editing studio for the chores that are known as post-production work. Then he bought a beach house at Malibu and converted his own Laurel Canyon house into a working headquarters. In bygone days, when Ashby was getting started in the business as a film editor, such work usually was done in dreary sheds that make the dark streets of some of the biggest movie studios resemble urban egg farms.

"I worked in those tiny rooms with those institutional green walls till I thought I'd go crazy," Ashby said. "And when you were working at a studio, all the editors who were out of jobs would stop by, looking for work. It was depressing to see ten friends who weren't working, and it was also hard to get any work done yourself."

What used to be a living room is now Ashby's office, with a king-size bed, littered with books and scripts, serving as his desk. To accommodate visitors, he located a couple of high-backed rolling office stools. The only real desk in the room, tucked into a corner beyond a projector-type TV set and giant TV screen, was occupied by a young man taking his phone calls.

The guru-like, above-it-all image of the mountaintop moviemaker was soon reinforced. All week long, in the Hollywood trade-paper columns, l'affaire *Shampoo* at the Golden Globe awards dinner had been subject of speculation. At the last minute, the cast of the film, including Warren Beatty, Julie Christie, Goldie Hawn, and Lee Grant, had canceled their reservations. Their prominent ringside table had to be filled with other celebrities so it wouldn't be empty during the nationwide telecast, and others had to take their places on the program as presenters. Could their director shed any light?

"I have to confess I didn't even know the Golden Globes were taking place Saturday night," Ashby said with a serene smile. "I didn't even know Julie was in town, and was surprised to hear that she was supposed to be there."

"All awards are kind of strange; because if you go along with the idea of winning, what you're basically doing is hoping somebody else will lose.

"When I won an Oscar for editing *In the Heat of the Night*, the biggest thrill I got out of it was my friends' reaction, because they seemed to be so pleased on my behalf, and I enjoyed that. But when I got nominated that year, I was really embarrassed because Dede Allen didn't get a nomination for *Bonnie and Clyde*, which I thought was a gross oversight.

"But Dede works in New York, you see, and all the academy voters are out here, and the New Yorkers don't get much consideration. Take Gordon Willis. He's the best cameraman in this country, but he's a New Yorker, and I don't know if he's ever been nominated."

Ashby recently finished filming *Bound for Glory*, based on Woody Guthrie's 1943 autobiography, with David Carradine playing the folk poet, singer, and author. Now, in former bedrooms a floor below, Ashby had film editors at work, assembling the movie. In a largish family-type room adjoining a patio, the walls were lined floor to ceiling with cans of *Bound for Glory* footage.

"For this picture, I shot about twice as much as I usually do," Ashby said. "There was a lot of action, and it just seemed the thing to do. I've just had to move my music editor into the garage.

The movie covers four years in Guthrie's life in the 1930s, when he drifted from Dust Bowl towns in Oklahoma and Texas to the migrant farmers' camps in California and then started making a name for himself in Los Angeles. Ashby built a period farm-workers' shantytown near Bakersfield and had the little California town of Isleton, near Stockton, dirtied up to resemble a run-down Texas town after a dust storm.

"Potentially, there's a lot of resemblance to *Grapes of Wrath*, because Woody was an Okie and that's pretty much his story," Ashby said. "I took a look at *Grapes of Wrath* before I started the film, just to make sure I wouldn't appear to be making a copy. Not that anybody could presume to make another *Grapes of Wrath*."

The director talked glowingly of his luck at finding good faces and lively, interesting extras in the farm areas where they shot the film. Also, at the height of the harvest season, he was staggered by such sights as truckloads of tomatoes, which he was normally accustomed to seeing only in supermarket-bin quantities.

"We lived very well with all that produce around us," he said.

Ashby said he uses the giant TV set as a casting tool:"When you're interviewing fifteen people a day, you can't really be fair to them all with one shot out, especially when you try to remember back to the ones you talked with early in the day. So now I make a videotape of every interview, or at least part of it. I have a video-cassette attachment and I can go back and put those faces up on the big screen, and it really helps.

"I ask my casting people to make tapes, too. I had this TV rig with me in Bakersfield, and instead of all the bother and expense of flying people up there for interviews, Lynn Stalmaster would talk with them here in L.A. and then send me cassettes.

"No, you don't tape Warren Beatty or Julie Christie, because you know their work. But for this picture I did make a tape of David Carradine. When I first talked with him, I had no idea I would use him.

I remember saying, 'Well, maybe if you were five feet ten, you'd have the part,' because Woody was a small man, and that's the way I was thinking. But then I began to understand that not enough people really know Woody that well, and the more I talked with David the more I knew his height wasn't important. So I made the tape mostly to show to the people at United Artists, who were putting up the money, just so they wouldn't think I was totally nuts. I had to get that *Kung-Fu* image of him out of their heads.

"David's musicianship was a part of it, too, although I didn't get more than about 60 percent of the musicianship I wanted out of him. Like a lot of actors, David gives his best musical performances away from the camera. But ultimately it doesn't make that much difference, because we're not making a musical. There are a lot of songs in the film, but I'm not certain that we'll hear any one song from start to finish.

"One of the problems with staging a musical scene is what else you put on the screen besides the song. You can show someone listening, but that's dangerous, because you have the person in the theater audience who says, 'Yes, well, that's what I'm doing.'"

Ashby said he hasn't tried to follow *Harold and Maude* with more wild comedy because he's been too interested in finding out how many other directions he can go.

"But I'll certainly do another one in that vein, because it's too much fun not to do," he said. Meanwhile, he's concerned with the gentler, slower-paced Okie humor that screenwriter Robert Getchell (*Alice Doesn't Live Here Anymore*) has captured in *Bound for Glory*.

"It has a different beat, and it took me a while to get used to it," Ashby said.

He led a brief tour through several editing rooms, where barefooted cutters were snipping away at some of the simulated Texas footage. Bob Jones, who is editing *Bound for Glory*, is another film editor who is being nudged upward on the moviemaking ladder by his boss, just as Ashby was nudged upward by director Norman Jewison after Ashby had edited a number of Jewison films, including *The Cincinnati Kid, The Russians Are Coming, the Russians Are Corning*, and *The Thomas Crown Affair*.

Jones has written the screenplay for Saul Bellow's *Henderson the Rain King*, one of the films Ashby intends to do next. Another script on Ashby's bed was a treatment by Richard Brautigan of his own novel, *The Hawkline Monster*.

"That one has been called a Gothic western," Ashby said. "I'm still not happy with the script. One way to go with it might be a wild *Harold and Maude* approach."

Hal Ashby Interview

Larry Salvato and Dennis Schaefer/1976

From *Millimeter*, October 1976. Reprinted with permission of Penton Media.

Hal Ashby sat with his legs crossed in a semi-yoga position. Behind him a row of windows bathed the room in a wispy, tree-filtered light. As he talked, Ashby calmly stroked his beard; he seemed very relaxed, very laid back, or, to use a term from the last decade, "mellow." There was no pretense here, none of the paranoid suspicion one often encounters in Hollywood. Success didn't seem to phase him much; after all, he is one of the top directors in the American motion picture industry, but you would never know it to look at him. No Gucci or turquoise, just bare feet and well-worn jeans with a sports jersey. His home-cum-office was equally simple; outside of the bed the most dominant fixture in the room was a video projection unit and screen.

Ashby's journey from Ogden, Utah, where he was born, to Lookout Mountain in the Hollywood Hills had been a long and difficult one. A product of a broken home, Ashby's early life was less than ideal. He didn't get along well with his family, hitchhiked to L.A. when he was seventeen, and was married and divorced twice before he was twenty-one. "I struggled towards growing up like most others, totally confused," Ashby reflected.

Finally at twenty-six, he got a job at Republic Studios running a multilith machine. Of all the odd jobs he had, this one was destined to leave its mark on him. "One day while running off thirty or so copies of some now-forgotten page 14, I flashed on the idea of becoming a film director," he said. After asking around about the best way to catapult from the multilith machine to the director's chair, most people told him, with typical Hollywood logic, to become an editor. Ashby, with a little luck in his corner, managed to get on as an apprentice editor only to find that he would have to toil for eight long years before he could become a full-fledged editor. Ashby commented that the union's eight-year rule "is a bad rule which tends to debilitate those who might have any creative juices going for them. It can become a full-out struggle just to hang on during those eight long years and some good talent has gone down the tubes in the process."

But in the long run, he believed that becoming an editor was good training, at least for him. "When the film gets to the editing room," said Ashby, "it's all there to be studied again and again." His first film as chief editor was *The Loved One*, but he only did the first cut on it; after which director Tony Richardson took it back to England to finish. Then another lucky thing happened. Ashby met Norman Jewison who was looking for an editor for *The Cincinnati Kid*. He got the job, but as it turned out, it was much more than that. Ashby edited Jewison's next three films and won an Academy Award for his work on *In the Heat of the Night*. After a while, Jewison boosted Ashby to the position of associate producer where he picked up more valuable experience. Then came a project called *The Landlord*, which Jewison was supposed to direct but couldn't because of a scheduling problem. Knowing Ashby's ambitions and goals, Jewison turned the film over to him and Hal Ashby, the director, was off and running. It only took fifteen years after operating that litho machine at Republic Studios, but Hal Ashby had finally arrived.

MM: From your work as an editor, did you learn anything about the relationship between the editor and director that helps you now that you are directing?

HA: Yes. Coming from my training I would never be an editor with any director who was going to stand over my shoulder, especially for the first cut. And the philosophy behind it is that it's another mind working on the film. Especially since all the editor is responding to is just the film. I never went out on locations, and I didn't want to know what the problems were. If it took you eight hours to get this particular shot because of this and that, I didn't care; what was important was what was happening on the piece of film. You put the film together and tell the story in the certain way you feel it from the film you have. And then you show and the worst thing that can happen—this actually happened to me when I was a director—is that it isn't any good. Then the best thing you can do is to put everything back into daily form. You can always put it back the way it was; that's the great thing.

I worked that way, and I would want any editor to work that way with me. I had a little bit of trouble with one editor who was trying to second-guess me, and there was a little bit of fear since I was known as a hot-shot editor. But that should never enter into it. And from my being an editor, I try to leave everything open. In other words, I don't camera cut; I leave everything as open as I can, because that provides more alternatives. The more alternatives you have the better, at least for my kind of filmmaking.

MM: So you tend to shoot a greater amount of film than one normally might?

HA: Yes, especially with an actor like Jack Nicholson. I will go for four or five takes on a thing, but what I really want him to do is four or five variations, slight variations that will work within the character and the context. Sometimes you intercut those takes, but what it does is leave you with the opportunity at the end, of saying, "That attitude in this take would be just a little bit better here than that attitude." It gives you choices.

MM: In your films the characters are usually very full and multifaceted. Do you consciously do anything to prevent your characters from becoming one-dimensional?

HA: I think it's mainly being aware of the fact that I don't want one-dimensional characters. I try to make my actors understand that. I think the great thing about features is that it allows you the time for a little more exploration. That doesn't mean walking around and thinking while everybody is waiting on the set. It's literally letting an actor get up and start working in front of you and then taking a look at it and saying, "What if we try it with this," or "That's too much." So that the actors will have a tendency to reach further and sometimes they might overreach. But by the very fact that they'll do that, it will usually come out. If a talented person takes a chance, nine times out of ten it will usually turn out pretty good. With people like Lee Grant and Jack Nicholson, if they do something in front of you, it's very rare that it's ever going to turn you off. With Jack I don't think he could ever do anything that would be too much. When I started *The Last Detail*, I watched him the first two or three days and he did some things that made me think, "Christ almighty, we'll never get away with this on film. It's just too big." But I didn't get into anything with him, because I wanted to see it on film first. It just felt too big, but when I looked at it, it wasn't. I've never seen anything like it. It was just a natural thing, and it never happens too big for film. I just had never seen it before, because there are limits with everybody else I've known. People like that help you explore these things and that way you get fuller characters.

MM: Your first two films weren't huge commercial successes, at least not initially. Did that have any effect on your career or the way you looked of things?

HA: No, I was very fortunate. When I started, it was very easy for me to do *The Landlord.* I had a great opportunity. Norman Jewison was so wonderful about setting that whole thing up; I never had to go through any of the battles on the financial level of it. I've been blessed with being very naive about certain things at a very late age in my life. It was very natural that I would go out and my first picture would be a two-million-dollar picture as opposed to a half-a-million-dollar picture. Because a half-a-million-dollar picture is hard to do in terms of making something work and come together. You have a better chance to make something work if you have two million dollars; you can be more full in what you want to tell.

The response to the film was very good in this town. In other words, people would look at it and wouldn't go into a thing about how much money it was making but rather how good a film it was. And that does happen. Now obviously if the film had been a big moneymaker, my whole life would have changed immediately. But I was still getting enough scripts from the time *The Landlord* was finished and released. So I settled right into looking for that which I really wanted to do. It wasn't a case of taking the first script that came along. So I wasn't negatively affected by it.

MM: You weren't originally involved in *Harold and Maude.* How did your participation come about? You were brought in late on it by Paramount?

HA: That's right. That script was sent to me by Bob Evans. I read it and liked it very much. I talked to Bob about it and said there were a lot of things I really liked about it but that I would like to sit and talk to the writer. Usually when you read a script and laugh out loud, that's a dangerous sign, because it's hard to translate to the screen. Bob also told me that Colin, the writer, was originally set to direct it. So I met with Colin and I got the whole story from him—about how the script was the thesis for his master's and how it was sold and how he was originally set to direct it. They gave him seven thousand dollars to shoot some tests, and the studio didn't like the tests. So I asked him if he were happy with the tests, and he said he still wanted to direct the film. So I went to Bob and took Colin with me. I told Bob that I couldn't do it and that he should let the man make his film. And Bob said, "Hal, if you don't do it, Colin is still not going to do it; somebody else will direct it." So I just asked Colin right there if he wanted me to do the film. I left it up to him. So Colin said he would like me to do it. Bob was really very good about it; he made it very clear that Colin would be a co-producer and he thought it would be good for Colin to be around me and watch and see what did. After I made the deal and looked at Colin's tests, I could see it was just a lack of experience and also he was a little bit too close to the material.

MM: How do you explain the cult status of *Harold and Maude*?

HA: I think it's because of what it has to say. It's the idea of the young and the old, the love thing, what she has to say, the statements and just the way the thing is presented. I think Bud [Cort] and Ruth [Gordon] are both wonderful in the film. Bud I've always been especially fond of because that's a tough role. There is nothing tougher than being the recipient of information and being made to look like Mr. Blah.

MM: Did the studio have a push behind it after its initial release or did the demand grow more by word of mouth?

HA: It grew. What happened is that the film has never been out of release. And that was the first way the studio could start to tell. The fact was they were always getting call-backs for this particular picture. So I think, on that level, what happened was there was a certain amount of business done and it probably affected different exhibitors in its own peculiar way. Because I know how everybody at Paramount reacted; they were really high on the film. So consequently the film has never been pulled to this day, over five years. Also, maybe it wasn't the exhibitors; maybe it was just enough people coming back and asking the theaters to play it again. It's probably been the most gratifying film I've ever made.

MM: In *Shampoo*, how much of the script was Warren Beatty and how much was Robert Towne? What was the level of collaboration?

HA: It was a pretty even thing as far as collaboration. Bob is the more complete writer because he's been writing more. The script had been around for a long, long time and he'd been involved with it for a long time. I had dinner with Warren one night and he said, "Did I ever tell you that it was originally titled *Hair*." It was *Hair* before *Hair* (on Broadway) was ever around, which was a great title for that too. So he told me the story behind it. Warren was working on *Bonnie and Clyde* and it took Bob a long time to write it, because Bob is a very thorough and thoughtful writer. But by the time he handed it in Warren was furious, because Bob had just been so long with it. So Warren saw everything that he thought was wrong with it, and, as Warren tells it, he sat down and started writing his own screenplay the day after.

So I said let me read both screenplays, and we'll sit down and talk about them. I read both of them, and I liked things in both of them. I could see what Bob had done and where Warren had gone. So got back to Warren and said that there was really something good here.

So Warren and I sat down for a couple of days and took pieces from both of them and put together a long rough composite kind of script. Then we asked Bob to come in and take a look at that and then we could sit down and go to work on it. So that's how it was; we all got into a room for about ten days. I acted more as a mediator, because they both had pride of authorship by then. So it was a close collaboration in that sense.

MM: It's surprising that it originally started out as a contemporary script; it really wasn't a period piece when it was first written?

HA: Right, the whole Nixon thing and all of that came in after the fact. In fact there was a whole thing about dope dealing in there, which at that time was contemporary. But by the time we got around to doing the picture, it was really way back there somewhere. So we didn't want to get into that and instead we wanted to go more for the political thing.

MM: Fifty years from now, when people see *Shampoo*, it will have more power just for the historical reference.

HA: That's right. That was all Warren's idea, by the way, the fact of the election eve/election day setting. We decided it would be just great never to show anybody voting or anything.

MM: What happened after you screened the film and then shortly afterwards the praise for the film was almost universal? Did you expect that?

HA: I never expect that on any film. I couldn't believe it. I was stunned by it. It got a couple of bad reviews like Nora Sayre in the *N.Y. Times*. Her review was so negative that it didn't make any sense, I mean, everything was wrong with the film, nothing was right with it. And I said, "Wait a minute, I can be off a little, but this is so extreme that I can't take it seriously." Then Canby came back and did a whole big thing on how great it was.

As far as where they (the critics) were, I really didn't have any idea, because there were so many elements in the picture to take off after— not in the quality of filmmaking and so forth but just in the characters themselves. I saw what that picture did when I ran it at the Director's Guild for an invited audience, where they bring their wives and so forth. All of them were getting up-tight; they thought we were present- ing Hollywood. It wasn't that at all. One person said to me afterwards that his wife said, "I know what that asshole (Beatty) is out doing all the time." And we weren't even presenting Hollywood people.

MM: People who live outside L.A. react to it differently than they do here.

HA: On that level, some people criticized it for the way we presented women in the film. We weren't trying to do anything except say that these were three women in this particular time and place; that's not the way a woman's to live by any means. That's not the way anybody should live, for Christ's sake; nobody should live the way those people did!

But audiences once you get outside L.A. and into Middle America, I can only think of them looking at it as a fantasy, saying, "Well, I'm sure that's the way they live out there." It's not anything they would comprehend as happening in their town.

MM: But those characters are very real, because they are very human. And that's something that shows up in all your films: the importance of human relationships and how people relate to each other. Is that something that you personally contribute to your films?

HA: It's just something I feel strongly about. When I first started mak- ing *The Landlord*, I wondered a lot about how much of me would come out on the screen. And after I was watching those dailies on the screen for a week, I was absolutely flabbergasted how much of me was coming out on the screen. It's just one of those things that happen if you feel strongly about something. And I am definitely responsible for it, and I would hope that I would never let it go any other way, because that's what is important: the human relationships and how people deal with each other.

But I think sometimes as far as commercial film making, it's very dangerous because it can get almost too subtle. In other words, you may get down to some really fine points where a general audience is not going to accept it because it doesn't have the climaxes it should have. How far can you go and still have an audience understand it? Talking about honesty on a commercial level, on *The Last Detail*, if we really wanted to go after the audience, the book had a much more commercial ending to it. Because what happened in the book was that both guys were so moved by what they had done that they went AWOL themselves. And in the end, Buddusky was killed by the shore patrol in Boston. That has more of a commerciality to it, because what you do is take the characters and make them what most people would like them to be.

What I settled on was that I can't believe that a guy who's in the Navy twelve years and another guy who's in for fourteen years will not only be affected by what they've done but both go AWOL; it's just beyond my belief. I don't believe it; show me one fucking guy who's done it. Maybe if he's in a war and killing people, you know, too much of it, one on top of another and more and more. This is a different experience and these guys are lifers. That's why to me, at the end, when Jack's walking along, talking and swearing about the grunts, he is as emotional as he can be and I felt he was affected. It's something that's going to be with him for the rest of his life. But to make so drastic a change, I wouldn't believe it. And I think the way we did it was more honest.

MM: Was there any flak from the studio the nature of the language, as far as selling the film to TV?

HA: After we'd finished shooting the picture, there was a period where the studio started getting very weird about the language. So one day we had a meeting at the studio and they said that they didn't want to emasculate the film but the language is very, very strong and we've got to do something about it. We want you to help us with it, because we feel we can reach a broader mass audience that way. So I said, "Wait a minute, you're telling me that if the word 'fuck' is used eighty times in the film and if we cut it down to forty times, we're going to reach a broader audience?" And they said, "Exactly." And I said, "I don't even know what the hell you're talking about, because I guarantee you now that the first time somebody opens his mouth and says 'fuck,' there's going to be ten people who get up and leave the theater. But if we do it and that just becomes part of it, maybe some people can actually have some fun with the picture, because that's the way these guys talk. So before we get into any of that, why don't we take the picture up to San Francisco and put it in a theater and look at it with an audience to see what happens?" So we previewed it in San Francisco and I don't think even ten people got up and left.

MM: Your new film, *Bound for Glory*, is a biography, which seems vastly different from your other films.

HA: It is and it isn't. It's biographical, but what I've ended up with is a film I could very well have made if it were fictitious. It deals with not too long a period of Woody Guthrie's life; primarily that period of time in which Woody absorbed a lot of information and started to become what he became, when he first started getting involved with unions, started writing songs, and made the migration from Texas to California. So it's a growing character.

But the film has been different in many respects. In a biography you run into a lot of things that you don't usually run into. It's very interesting to be on the set shooting a story about Woody Guthrie and having one of his wives and some of his children from different marriages there. It's interesting to see how they feel, especially Mary, his first wife, who is portrayed in the film.

MM: Did you feel restricted because you were dealing with a real person and real events?

HA: No. I took the license that I felt I had to take with the picture. For instance, I never tried to make David Carradine look like Woody or sound like Woody. I thought that would be dangerous, because he isn't Woody. He has the *spirit* of Woody closer than anybody else I ran into and that's all I ever went for. If those people (Woody's family and friends) didn't like that, there was nothing I could do about it. At the same time, they're anxious to see Woody become more well-known.

The real hard-core Woody Guthrie freaks may not like the film that much, but you've got to make the picture for other people that will come to it and say, "Hey, I didn't know about that; I didn't know about Woody Guthrie; that's fantastic." That's what I want people to get out of it, because Woody was great; he wrote great songs.

MM: How did you first get involved with the project?

HA: They mentioned it to me at United Artists. They said they had this screenplay of Robert Getchell's and it had to do with Woody Guthrie. And I just immediately said that it sounded terrific. I didn't even have to read the screenplay, because I just felt so strongly about doing a story about Woody Guthrie. I knew a lot about Woody already, but I didn't know that much about him, not nearly as much as when I got into the project and started reading.

MM: What kind of people did you initially consider for the Guthrie role?

HA: Oh my God, I was all over the place; I was everywhere. In fact, I was working with Tim Buckley for a while before Tim died. We were stunned, because we were going to get together with him the next day. I have a tape of him here that he made four days before he died.

So, I've gone that way, thinking about singers and that kind of thing. Also, Tim had a lot of that spirit too and he physically looked more like Woody because of his size and stature. Naturally I thought about Arlo Guthrie, but I didn't think Arlo was quite the actor that would be required. That plus the strain of doing his father. He'd say no, there wouldn't be any strain at all, but there's got to be a certain thing there of actually doing that which made me back away from it. It's endless, the ways I went to cast Woody.

I'd never met David Carradine before. We just met when he came to call, saying he would like to sit down and talk with me about it. He came and we sat down; I thought it would be about fifteen or twenty minutes, but we spent an hour and a half just rapping and talking about different things. Still, six weeks later, I hadn't decided, but he just kept popping back up. He had two things going for him. He had a good rural look, whatever that is exactly; and the other thing was this spirit, an attitude.

MM: *Bound for Glory* seems less commercial than any of your previous films.

HA: It might and might not be. I'm not sure.

MM: In other words, you're taking more of a risk this time with this kind of subject?

HA: Yes, definitely we're taking much more of a risk. God knows, Woody had a lot to say to people. I'm now toying with the idea of dropping some of the speech-making out of the film, because I don't like speech-making. But at the same time, it's the only film I've ever made where it's legitimate for someone to get up and really say something. Because that's what he did. So I've shot some of those things and basically they work quite well. Woody took some definite stands, you know what I mean; he was more or less talking about greed and saying it straight out.

Gambling on a Film about the Great Depression

Aljean Harmetz/1976

From the *New York Times*, December 5, 1976, © 1976 The New York Times. All rights reserved. Used by permission and protected by the Copyright Laws of the United States. The printing, copying, redistribution, or retransmission of the Material without express written permission is prohibited.

Barefoot and wearing frayed gray corduroy pants, director Hal Ashby sits in the $350,000 beach house that *Shampoo* bought for him. He wore the same pants yesterday, unaware of the hole in the back, and will probably wear them tomorrow. Forty-five-year-old Hal Ashby has little in common with the smooth, cruel, brittle, expensively dressed characters in his most famous movie.

Two days later, Ashby will have to put on shoes—for the first time in a week—and comb his yellow-gray goat's beard and his wild hair and accompany his new movie, *Bound for Glory*, to New York. *Bound for Glory*, a $7,000,000 biography of folk singer Woody Guthrie, is not nearly so secure a commercial venture as slick and exhibitionistically sexy *Shampoo*. A memoir of the Depression, *Bound for Glory* is no road-map through Woody Gutherie's life with occasional pauses to watch him rush to his guitar and compose a song. In fact, almost no song is heard whole within the film because Ashby did not want to make a standard "boring" musical biography. The movie focuses on the four years between 1936 and 1940 when Guthrie (played by David Carradine), increasingly radicalized, walks out on his family to pour his love and his music onto factory workers and migrant laborers. It is a portrait of an uncomfortably ambiguous man, a fact of which Ashby is well aware. "If you want to make a Woody Guthrie film that is solidly commercial you have to have someone kill him in the end."

Ashby chews a piece of sugarless gum and stares at the ocean through red-tinted glasses with thin steel rims. He is tall and thin with a long face and crooked teeth. He has been a vegetarian for eight years. He stopped eating meat after a series of nightmares in which animals were killed to provide him with food.

"You wouldn't typecast Hal as a film director," says cinematographer Haskell Wexler. "Most directors are dictatorial, active managerial, executive types. Hal's gentle."

"We were more concerned with who would direct *Bound for Glory*, than with who would play Woody," says the picture's producer, Robert Blumofe. "Hal was my first choice, the big piece of the jigsaw puzzle. Because he cares about people. He cared about me. If most directors give you a year, you're lucky. Hal was on a flat deal and no matter how long he worked on the film, he didn't get any more money. But he put in close to two years on the picture, despite the fact that his agents were pushing for him to 'make more bread.'"

Ashby's willingness to spend two years on *Bound for Glory* may merely be because—having been a movie director for six years—he is still surprised to be one at all. He was forty by the time he became a director, nineteen years after he had gone to the California State Department of Unemployment and naively asked for a job in a movie studio. There had, incredibly, been a job available, for a multilith (a kind of mimeograph machine) operator. It took him five years to become an apprentice film editor, fifteen years to become an Academy Award-winning film editor for Norman Jewison's *In the Heat of the Night.*

By that time, he says, "I'd been working seventeen hours a day, seven days a week for ten years. I'd wake up at 3 A.M. and go to work. I'd try to leave the studio at 6 and still be there at 9. I'd gotten better and better at my work, meanwhile wrecking three marriages. Suddenly, I was tired. I'd become a film editor because everyone said it was the training for a director. But suddenly I was almost forty, and I no longer had the energy to pursue it. So I stopped."

Then, in 1970, Jewison found himself unable to direct *The Landlord* and handed it over to Ashby. Ashby followed *The Landlord* with *Harold and Maude, The Last Detail, Shampoo,* and *Bound for Glory*. Until recently—until the box office success of *Shampoo*—he did not have the kind of power that allows a director to pick material congenial to his view of the world. Even so his films share a common kindness toward their characters, a sense that being one's brother's keeper makes mortality a little more bearable. It is partly that gentleness in portraying the love between an eighty-year-old woman and a neurotic twenty-year-old that made *Harold and Maude* into a cult film. Ashby even finds it necessary to be kind to characters who displease him. "I didn't like the people in *Shampoo*. And the career sailors in *The Last Detail*. I don't like the idea of people doing that with their lives. But I wouldn't take any cheap shots at them. I felt sorry for them." If nobody quite uses the word "saintly" when referring to Ashby, they discuss him, as his friend Jack Nicholson says, "like we're writing a recommendation for a college scholarship." He is, says Warren Beatty, "a good man." "Most movie companies drive the wagons right over the grave," says Nicholson. "Hal delayed the start of *The Last Detail* for a week so an actor could come to terms with the knowledge he had a terminal illness." It is doubtful whether Ashby's five ex-wives would exactly agree, after years of putting dinner on the table at 6 and having him arrive home at 10. But then, "I understood Woody Guthrie very well," says Ashby, referring to Guthrie's ability to love the whole world while running out on his wife and two daughters.

Ashby sips a glass of water and eats a handful of raw nuts, looking much too unassuming for a man who has five ex-wives. A number of thin, blonde girls with heart-shaped faces walk through the house on their way to or from the water's edge. He is, at the moment, unattached. He finishes the water and pours himself some apple juice. Except for an occasional glass of tequila or wine, he stopped drinking alcohol ten years ago. "I was a great drinker and one morning I woke up and decided I was poisoning myself." Nor does he drink coffee or tea anymore.

What is most surprising—given the compulsions that made him work seventeen hours a day and that have prevented him from taking a vacation in the last four years—is the lack of tension he projects. He had to move out of his last house because he had filled it so full of editing equipment—so that he could roll out of bed at 3 A.M. and go to work—that there was hardly any place left to sleep. But he is as loose, as limp, as unthreatening as a rag doll. It is, perhaps, this lack of ego, combined with his great technical skill, that has caused people in Hollywood to extend themselves in unaccustomed ways: made Norman Jewison hand him a picture to direct, made United Artists' Arthur Krim agree to go ahead with *Bound for Glory* even when no name actor was available to play Guthrie.

That was April 1975, and both Dustin Hoffman and Jack Nicholson had turned down the role. Hoffman had been worried about a role which required him to sing and play the guitar. Nicholson had chosen to take the opportunity of working with Marlon Brando in *The Missouri Breaks*. For a while after that, it seemed as though nobody suitable would ever be found. Richard Dreyfuss was almost offered the part. Tim Buckley died of a drug overdose a few days before he would have been offered it. David Carradine was interviewed and dismissed. He was, among other things, too tall. "But I kept thinking about him," says Ashby, "and, in July, I called him back. He had the right rural look and musicianship. And he had a 'to hell with you' attitude, but it did cause me some problems. Once, when we were doing a scene, some migrant workers marched by. David started marching with them. By the time we found him, he was two miles away; and he had held up shooting for three hours."

There is no anger in Ashby's voice as he relates the incident. He is willing to accept almost anything that makes an actor more comfortable. "His point of view hasn't been engraved in stone." says Nicholson of Ashby. "He has such a light touch that some people who have worked with him aren't even sure he's directed the picture." Ashby admits that he is "not as tyrannical as most directors. I don't visualize myself as 'the boss.' What I try to do is get as much creativity as possible from every person I'm working with. Haskell Wexler drives some directors crazy because he feels strongly about everything. I love to have him around. He's my conscience. But in the end I make the decision—to turn the camera on; to turn the camera off."

Some of Ashby's lack of tyranny comes from what Wexler calls "his genius as an editor. So much of filmmaking happens after the shooting stops. The shooting of the film is like the top of the iceberg. There are hidden secrets in film which Hal can uncover. He has enormous technical skill in mixing, editing, dubbing."

Because of his skill in assembling film, Ashby can afford to experiment. What frightens him most is the possibility "of becoming too rigid with film, of seeing it all so clearly in my head in advance that it's no longer real, of concentrating on who's going to walk here and who's going to walk there." One result of Ashby's untidy openness is an extraordinary sense of relationship between his characters. Except for *Shampoo*, they do not shout at each other from across the screen but seem to be bound by an elastic band that will continue to hold them after the cameras have been turned off. Ashby is "aware that the actors are connecting." He thinks it is "a question of honesty. If I catch an actor at all uncomfortable with the dialogue, it means it's not honest to him. So I'll change it."

Bound for Glory does not match "the unattainable perfect picture" inside Ashby's head. He is disturbed by some of the speeches, particularly by a scene where migrant worker Randy Quaid tells Guthrie to "keep on singing." (That scene was restored by United Artists executives after Ashby had cut it. After seeing Ashby's three-hour version, they missed several scenes in his tighter final cut and asked him to reinsert them. It is usual Hollywood procedure for a director to be asked to make his picture shorter.) But what Ashby believes he has achieved is the authentic re-creation of America. "It's like we stepped out the door and into 1937," he says.

Ashby remembers 1937, remembers his father loading his milk wagon and taking the milk down to a hobo camp in Ogden, Utah. That was after his parents had left the Mormon Church, after they were divorced, and before the dairy was lost because his father refused to accept pasteurization of milk. Six years later his father placed a rifle underneath his chin and pulled the trigger. "I was twelve years old. My father used to make me laugh a lot. He would give me a dollar for taking the soda pop bottles to the basement of the store. But we didn't know each other. And only now, in retrospect, can I see how much pain he must have been in." Of all Ashby's films, *Bound for Glory*—with its raw Southwestern hero and its uneasy questions about love—is closest to his own life. There is even a scene—in which David Carradine, hitchhiking to California, sleeps all night at the edge of the highway—which comes not from Guthrie's past but from Ashby's.

He was seventeen years old, already once married and divorced. It was September and he was repairing concrete railroad bridges in Wyoming. "It was only September and it was already so cold there were two inches of ice on the water barrel. I broke the ice, took a drink, and said to my friend, 'I'm going to California and live off the fruit of the land.' I packed my suitcase, but I left my work clothes behind. Outside Provo, Utah, I slept all night by the side of the road. The next day a deer hunter, the deer tied to the fender, gave me a ride all the way to L.A."

Three weeks later, he took his last dime and called his mother collect to ask for help. Ashby had been born when his mother was forty-four, his oldest brother almost twenty. His mother herself was the result of a polygamous marriage. Ashby's grandfather had had five wives, keeping one in town, one on his ranch, three on his farms. By nature or necessity a rigid woman, she turned her youngest son down. Ashby took the dime and bought a Powerhouse candy bar. The candy bar lasted for three days—on the fourth day he found a job.

Originally, Ashby wanted a job in a movie studio because "it seemed glamorous." Now, he says diffidently, he hopes his films "will have something to do with the human condition." By that, he means "dealing with what people have the most trouble with, the relationships between them." Pinned across one wall of an upstairs bedroom are the photographs published in *Life* magazine of the 242 young men who died during one week of the Vietnamese war. In January he will start shooting *Coming Home*, a movie about the survivors of that war.

Ashby describes himself most often as "naive," and he says now, with naiveté and uncalculated charm, that "it is a wonderful thing to look at your work and not be embarrassed by it."

That Special Okie Southwest Flavor, That Humor

David Sterritt/1977

Reproduced with permission from the February 4, 1977 issue of *The Christian Science Monitor* (www.CSMonitor.com). © 1977 The Christian Science Monitor.

A room with Hal Ashby in it is a cheery one.

An aura of faintly old-fashioned hipness hovers about his faded corduroy pants, tie-dyed T-shirt, and brightly flowing hair, and his chuckly voice erupts constantly in a laugh that's really a gleeful hoot. You'd be happy too if you'd directed such hits as *Shampoo*, *The Last Detail*, and followed them with the critically acclaimed *Bound for Glory*.

I first met Ashby in Stockton, California, as he shot *Bound for Glory* with David Carradine. I was scheduled to arrive at the location on a Monday, but United Artists eagerly suggested I come several days earlier to watch the shooting of an "amazing freight-train scene." So I revised a complicated cross-country itinerary—airline tickets, accommodations, ground transportation—and showed up at the recommended time. Ashby shook my hand, pointed out cinematographer Haskell Wexler, and clambered to the top of a freight car, which promptly took off into the distance, not to return for several hours. So much for the "amazing freight-train scene."

A Chat Develops

Now at last I'm chatting with Ashby in the civilized confines of a New York hotel suite, and he hoots as I recall my Stockton visit (which in the end I spent profitably watching Carradine learn to play the fiddle). Ashby is delighted with the way *Bound for Glory* turned out, and hopes it will reach "as broad an audience as possible." How does one go about recruiting such an audience? "I have no idea," is the response.

Bound for Glory tells of Woody Guthrie's early years as a folk singer, social activist, and all-round ramblin' man. The Robert Getchell script is based on portions of Guthrie's autobiography of the same title. Though it reflects many of the social tensions and struggles of the depression years, Ashby sees it as "more naïve than political. It's about learning processes and character, so young people will probably identify with it faster, because that's where you are at a certain stage of your life. But older people are drawn to the movie too, if they've been through any part of that '30s experience."

Okie Rhythm Hailed

Ashby regards the *Glory* book as "a fantastic piece of work, and written by a very young man. Its flavor was definitely an influence on the film; at least I hope it's there—that Okie Southwest rhythm, and that special humor. We wanted to capture that *texture*."

Does the movie succeed, in his view? "I talked to Woody's family and people who knew him. I wanted to know what sense they'd get out of it. I tried for the spirit of Woody and people say we caught it—after five minutes they forget it's Davie on screen. . . . This was important for me, because I didn't want one of those things where the family's running around angry."

Paradoxically, the story of folksy Woody cost a whopping $7 million to film. Shooting lasted nearly five months, going six weeks over schedule. Most of the extra money went for period authenticity, as in huge "Hooverville" migrant camps. "I always felt it was a very intimate story," explains the director, "but it had to be against a big canvas. And it just kept getting bigger."

Since *Bound for Glory* is Ashby's fifth feature since leaving his post as one of Hollywood's top film editors, I ask if he feels any connective tissues running through his work. "There's no story line or anything like that running through my pictures," he answers, "but I try to do films that deal with human relations, with people relating to one another. Which apparently a lot of people are not into doing these days."

Different Love Story

This concern with people rather than sharks or giant apes will be evident in the next Ashby project, *Coming Home*—a "different kind of love story, where a woman falls in love with a paraplegic." It will star Jane Fonda, Bruce Dern, and Jon Voight in a Vietnam-era setting. Next, probably, will come a movie version of Richard Brautigan's *The Hawkline Monster: A Gothic Western*. This novel seems impossibly slight and repetitious to me, but Ashby insists "it will work on film, even though I've never seen anything like it before. It has two hysterical, unusual, fascinating characters. . . ."

Looking back on his beginnings in Hollywood, Ashby remembers them as unspectacular. "I was a kid looking for something," he reminisces, "but I didn't know what. The movie business seemed like a terrific thing to get into. I'd go into the unemployment office and say I wanted to start at the bottom. People love to hear that, though of course I didn't want to start at the bottom anymore than anybody else. Finally I got this weird job copying scripts at Universal Pictures."

"I looked around, and directing looked like the best gig. So I tried to become an assistant director, but I found out that editing was a better 'school.' It took three years to get a job as an apprentice editor, and it was a great school, though time-consuming. My life changed when I met [director] William Wyler and some of the others. Then all the doors opened, like in a movie. And Norman [*In the Heat of the Night*] Jewison was a good man, I could tell I was a good editor for him, because I could see the load I took off him."

Hand Fairly Free

Today Ashby can pretty well write his own ticket, especially in the wake of *Shampoo*, a depiction of dreary sensuality which remains the biggest moneymaker in Columbia Pictures history. ("For them, not for me," muses Ashby with a rather muted hoot.) Interestingly, this young celebrity among directors doesn't think today's movies hold up against Hollywood works of the past.

"Back in the old studio days—which I didn't go through, remember—the studios owned the theaters, so their main need was for lots of 'product.' They had to be factories, but they made better, more controversial films. The less expensive 'B' pictures were great breeding grounds for directors, including former editors. And you could do films that had more to say, because there were just more films.

"Now if you have something to say you have to gamble $4–$5 million, at a time when business isn't that good. Everybody's trying to play it safer, to protect the investment and take care of the corporation."

Treading the Middle

Ashby's own films have managed to tread a careful line down the middle, making their statements and sometimes innovating while keeping an eye on the mainstream audience. While his works may disappoint, at times, they are painstakingly crafted by a self-admitted "slow cutter" who used to sit fourteen to eighteen hours a day in the editing room "until I realized there must be more to life than this." Now he works with another editor (often a fast one) and concentrates most of his attention on overseeing the assemblage of scenes.

He is a serious filmmaker, and his movies show it. But listen closely and you'll hear echoes of that hooting Ashby laugh refusing to take itself too seriously. Which is a healthy thing in any business.

Hal Ashby

Tay Garnett/1977

From *Directing: Learn from the Masters*, by Tay Garnett, edited by Anthony Slide, Scarecrow Press, 1996. Reprinted with permission of Rowman & Littlefield Publishing Group.

1. What was your personal background (your vocation) before entering this field of endeavor?

I've had very many jobs. I traveled around just trying to find what I wanted to do. This is prior to getting into the motion picture field, and becoming a director. I finally got into film editing. I was a film editor for about ten years and found it to be an excellent background.

2. What was your first position in the movie business? Were you an assistant director, a cameraman, an actor, a writer, a film editor, an agent, or other? Please indicate the steps that led to your directing.

My first position was running a copy machine making copies of scripts at Universal. I got that job from the State Employment Office in Van Nuys. I went there because it was a free employment agency. I remember sitting there, waiting for about an hour. I told the lady who interviewed me that I wanted to get into the film industry. She looked at me like I was crazy.

From there, I wanted to become a director. I thought, at that time, the quickest way to directing was to become an assistant director, but everyone I spoke to said, "Get into editing. With editing, everything is up there on film for you to see over and over again. You can study it and ask why you like it, and why you don't."

All this took a long time. The biggest break came for me when, after two years, I worked with William Wyler on *The Big Country* [1958]. I was, like, the fifth assistant on it. Those people opened all the doors for me. They really encouraged everyone to get their ideas out. What a blessing it was; the experience changed my life.

3. What is your philosophy regarding your film: your aim or purpose in making it? Is there an underlying objective beyond providing entertainment?

My philosophy is what I like to call preoccupation with the "human condition," which can, of course, mean a lot of things. It's basically the relationship between people. I like to do that with entertainment. I just can't get into the idea of pure entertainment. If something is really good, even if someone approaches it with pure entertainment in mind, I think it will have an underlying theme. If I'm dealing with characters that I don't particularly like, I try to be kind with them. If I like the characters, I'm very hard on them.

4. In seeking a story on which to base a film, in what particular genre do you hope to find it?

I look everywhere for my source material. It doesn't matter what genre it might be. Whatever comes along that interests me, I'll do.

5. Have you a preference as to the source of your story material: story or script written directly for the screen, a play designed for theatrical use, or a story (fact or fiction) intended for book or magazine publication? Please explain reasons for your choice.

I believe an original story would be my preference, because it starts right out with the idea of film in mind. I find that I have to read a script two or three times to fully understand it and bring it to life.

Other things happen with novels; I find I get too emotionally involved in reading a novel. Transposing that to a screenplay is difficult.

A short story might be interesting, and that's one thing I haven't done.

I think there's very little relationship between the stage play and film. I think the best thing you can hope for out of a stage play is to get some very highly emotional things like the delivery of dialogue.

6. In any of the above cases, do you prefer using another screen dramatist to prepare the actual shooting script, or do you choose to do that work yourself?

I prefer to use another screenplay writer. I like that input, and objective viewpoint.

7. If you do use another scriptwriter, do you like to work closely with him (or her) as a co-writer, or do you elect to allow the writer to express his views fully, then ultimately do the final script polish yourself?

I let them have as much freedom to create as they need, and I will sit with them at the end, and use what I want. I've found with film that the more creativity you can get out of other people, the better chance you have of making a good film.

8. Does it please you to have all the action (business) worked out fully on paper before you start shooting, or do you prefer to improvise?

The structure of the script is very important to me, so I don't start messing around with that while I'm shooting. If a scene isn't working, I might get into improvisation as long as I know what the obligation of the scene is. I like the spontaneity of films, so I don't like to get it down exactly as the script reads.

9. Is there one specific component involved in the creation of a film, which you regard as transcendent in importance: story, script (or scriptwriter), star or stars, cast (as a whole), film editor, art director, or cameraman?

All of them. The guard is just as important as the quarterback. It's a communal operation to make a film.

10. Do you work with a producer? If "Yes": what functions do you expect from him? If "No": would you care to explain?

The function I expect from the producer is to try to get me what I need, and to take a lot of pressure off me. On a more important level, I want that producer's creative input, because he usually feels as close to that story or film as I do, and should have a lot of things to say about it. I look for those things to be said. I expect to have him take care of all the business end of things. Also, I try very hard to work with my producers.

If I were a producer and director on my own films, I would get a sensational production manager and let him become, in effect, an associate producer, and let him produce the film himself.

11. Do you use a dialogue director, if only to save time by making sure that all the actors know their lines? Or, if you use one, is it because you feel that he brings other values to your operation? Kindly elucidate.

I haven't used a dialogue director yet.

12. Do you like to have your writer or producer on your set while you are rehearsing or shooting?

That's entirely up to them. If the writer or producer would like to be on the set, they're more than welcome. Certainly with *Shampoo* [1975], Robert Towne was on the set most of the time, along with Warren Beatty.

13. Do you work closely with your cameraman prior to shooting: planning effective dramatic and mood lighting, predetermining every camera set-up for effectiveness dramaturgically as well as composition-wise, and in blocking out all camera movements in minute detail? Or, do you again prefer to extemporize?

I don't block out my camera movements in advance. I work very closely with the cameraman before shooting and we talk concept of the overall look of the film; at that time we sometimes make a test to have something concrete to look at. Sometimes he'll make the set-up to see if I like it, and if it feels comfortable.

When we start shooting I'm probably closer to my cameraman than anyone else in the crew. I always make sure I ride to work with him, or come home with him, so we can talk. I've found that the more freedom a cameraman has, the better he works.

14. How closely do you supervise the casting of your films? Do you pay particular attention to the proper casting of the more important roles, then allow your casting director to set the other parts, or do you maintain rigid control of setting the entire cast, down to the one-line bit parts?

I maintain a tremendous control on casting. I work very closely with my casting director. Casting is one of the toughest things in the film for me. Casting the major roles can become really frustrating, because it's the first major decision. You have human beings out there waiting to get work.

On *Bound For Glory* [1976], I used my Advent television screen and my video recorder! I had my casting director, Lynn Stalmaster, tape interviews with all the one-liners and one-day players. I was shooting in Stockton and Bakersfield, so he would send the tapes up to me at night. I could play them, run them back and forth until I got a good look. It was a good technique, because those being tested were far more comfortable with the casting director than they would have been with me.

15. In considering actors, do you prefer working with the seasoned "technician," or with the more "instinctive" type? Would you care to express your views toward the "method actor"?

I have no preference. When an actor is good all I know is that I get excited. Whatever it takes for the actor to get where he or she wants to go, it doesn't matter to me how it's done, as long as it works. But he has to have some of the instinct. I do, too. One can have all the "method" there is, but if the instinct isn't there, it's nothing.

16. Is it your practice, before rehearsals—even before the actor has had a chance to form his own image of the character or to absorb his lines—to discuss with him, in depth, your concept of the character or the relationship of that part to the play-structure as a whole? Or is it your position that, having chosen the actor, you would be better advised to let him exercise, uninhibited, those qualities for which you selected him, thus allowing for the possibility of his bringing to the characterization, a plus which is entirely his own?

I believe that actors are intelligent people and are capable of giving a character more study, more thought, and more levels than I ever could. If they're good actors, they'll explore many different ways. Take Jack Nicholson in *The Last Detail* [1973]; before shooting, we talked about five or ten different approaches to his character. We talked concept. I never want that exploration to stop. I always encourage my actors to look at the dailies.

Again, with Jack, if he noticed some little mannerism he did, and it worked, he would continue to do it. It was much easier with Jack sitting there with me than if I approached him the next day and said, "You know that little thing you did yesterday . . . "

17. Some very fine directors believe in long rehearsals, covering the entire script with the complete cast, as one would in a theatrical production. Others, perhaps equally talented, shun this method on the theory that "Too much rehearsal flattens out spontaneity." Many hold their rehearsals to a minimum, on the theory that by "shooting rehearsals" they avoid the possibility of leaving the player's best performance on the rehearsal hall floor. What is your view on this subject?

I'm more for spontaneity. I think rehearsals are good if you have something complicated that needs to be worked out. It's best to work things out on a Sunday, before you start shooting on Monday morning. That's better than, say, working out something eight weeks in advance, then—ready to shoot—you're standing on the set saying, "Gee—what was it we did eight weeks ago?"

18. Do you insist that an actor adhere meticulously to the script—lines and business—or do you accept the position of some very able actors, that a slight change here or there, can damage nothing, but will enable them to bring more realism, color or effectiveness to the character being portrayed?

What ever more color and realism an actor can bring to a script with slight alterations, I'm for. Considering the number of people involved in making a film, it doesn't make much sense to insist that every word must be spoken exactly as it was written.

19. To what extent do you supervise the editing of your film? Note: I recall one director—one of the all-time great American Directors—who loathed viewing his own rushes. He preferred to allow his editor to make his own first rough cut. Then the director would move in and live with the film until a final editing was achieved that presented the picture to a viewer precisely as he had intended as he shot it.

Will you kindly express your views as to the importance of this phase of picture-making, and your individual approach to it?

I do like to look at my dailies. I let the editor have free reign to put the stuff together in a way about which he feels strongly. I did that myself as an editor. It all has to do with getting maximum creativity out of all the elements involved in making a film.

Nowadays, an innovation helps: we have those tabletop editors that are just fantastic. I was raised on the old moviola. I started to use the tabletop on *Harold and Maude* [1971].

20. How vital do you believe the musical score to be, as an adjunct in emphasizing the emotional, dramatic, or comedic values of a picture?
The musical score is vital, I think. You just have to be careful not to overdo it.

21. Are you deeply involved in the preparation and recording of the musical score for your films? Note: Obviously we are not dealing with filmed opera or musical comedy at this point.
I'm very much involved, at least in discussion of what I feel the music should be. I usually find records, and track a portion, a melody or a theme—not to guide or hamper the composer's freedom—but to give him an inkling of what I'm trying for. Over a period of time, I've had the opportunity to experiment with a number of different musical approaches.

22. Do you exercise final control as to which scenes are to be scored, and which are to be played a capella?
Do you have a fixed rule by which you determine this for yourself? If so, would you care to elaborate?
I have no fixed rule. I usually sit with the composer and pick the areas where I think we should have music. Most composers won't get too alarmed if you should drop something (that they've done) when you get to the mix.

23. We who have directed silent pictures are inclined, perhaps, to overestimate the importance of sound effects, particularly in action sequences. What is your viewpoint on this? To what extent do you participate in the recording and dubbing of the sound effects in your films?
Because I've come out of the editing field, I've been very fortunate in knowing some very good sound effect editors, and I've been lucky enough to get them on my films. I know I'm going to have an excess of what I need, but the fact stands that sound effects are very important to the film.

After you have completed the questionnaire, if you feel that you have left unsaid, anything that you believe could be vital to the growth and development of the Student Director, please write whatever you have in mind, as fully as you can spare time to do it.

It is quite possible that such thoughts from a man of your standing might well exercise tremendous influence on the lives and careers of a number of future filmmakers.

I'd like to impress the importance of a certain openmindedness to be maintained by a newcomer toward the thoughts and ideas of others. Don't ever limit yourself to saying, "This is exactly what I want. You move here, you move there, and speak these words." The result tends to be "locked in" and rigid. On *Harold and Maude* Colin Higgins, the author, was supposed to direct the film.

I went to Robert Evans and said, "Let Colin direct."

Evans said, "No."

I left it up to Colin, who was sitting beside me, as to whether he wanted me to direct the film.

He said I was to do it; Colin was made co-producer; in that capacity, he was able to remain on the set and watch the film being made.

There were times when it was really hard for him to stand by and watch the necessary changes being made. I would say to him, "Try to keep an open mind about these things." He tried, but it wasn't easy.

Then, by the time we got into the editing, he began to understand why certain things were done and why certain other things were not done. I think he was pleased with the result.

So, in making films, it's very important to keep an open mind.

Positive Thinking

Ralph Appelbaum/1978

From *Films and Filming*, July 1978. Reprinted with the permission of Ralph Appelbaum.

Hal Ashby, director of the first magnitude, is at the exclusive Carlyle Hotel in New York, talking on the 'phone with his agent. He is fervent, vigorous, and sparkles his speech with a jubilant glee, because even though the agent hasn't set a deal for the next film, there is a wealth of material to sort out and choose from, and the prediction that *Coming Home*, Ashby's latest film, is going to outgross *Shampoo*, which thus far has done twenty-two million dollars in rentals.

When I visited Ashby at the Carlyle, he was, as usual, barefoot and wearing corduroy jeans and a plaid shirt—his work clothes. Certainly not the image one conjures up of the Hollywood director. But then, Ashby has never been 100 percent establishment, and his films reflect—whether it be *Harold and Maude*, in which a twenty-year-old rich boy falls in love with an eighty-year-old woman, or *Bound for Glory*, the story of folk singer Woody Guthrie—his scepticism of human nature and the unique ways people cope with success and failure.

Coming Home, which some reviewers have labelled his best film, was a picture five years on the drawing board, one which almost every studio gave the thumbs-down to, and it is only due to Jane Fonda's persistence that the picture has seen the light of day. But one can understand the studios' reluctance to finance such a product. After all, the Vietnam war, which this film chronicles, was a national embarrassment to the American public; it cost thousands of lives, a fortune to fight, and it broke up families and divided the nation. People may not want to re-live such a trauma, and the studios did not want to take the gamble. Until now, of course. Because there are a half-dozen or so Vietnam-orientated films scheduled for release in the coming year, one being Francis Ford Coppola's long-awaited *Apocalypse Now*.

But Ashby's movie is, like *The Best Years of Our Lives*, more a love story, or character study, than a war film, because there are no battle scenes. It's about the battle on the homefront and what happens when a woman falls in love with a paraplegic, a so-called "War Hero," while her husband, a Marine captain, is overseas fighting a war "because it's expected of him." It's about changes, about growing up, about facing responsibilities and learning to live with one another, and it's told with honesty and compassion, two ingredients one sees throughout Ashby's work. Jane Fonda, Jon Voight, and Bruce Dern play the woman, the paraplegic, and the captain, respectively.

Today, Ashby is what's known as a "hot" director, and his attachment to a particular film property is all that's needed to get the cameras rolling. But it wasn't always that way, and Ashby is not one to forget the fifteen long and difficult years it took him to rise to the ranks of director.

Born in Ogden, Utah, Ashby's childhood was not an entirely happy one. He didn't get along with his family (his parents were divorced when he was five or six), and dropped out of high school in his senior year to hitchhike to Los Angeles. He was married and divorced twice before he was twenty-one.

Eventually, he found work as a multilith operator at the Republic Studios, and it was while running off ninety or so copies of some page 14, he says, that the idea of becoming a film director flashed upon him. And when he queried those around him for advice, the most common remark was: "The best school for a director is in the cutting room."

Luckily, Ashby had a friend who hired him as an apprentice editor, which led to a meeting with editor Bob Swink and work on *The Big Country*, *The Diary of Anne Frank*, *The Young Doctors*, *The Children's Hour*, *The Greatest Story Ever Told*, and others. But his first solo effort came eight years later, because of a union rule which demands you work that length of time as an apprentice, when he cut *The Loved One* for director Tony Richardson. But because Richardson had commitments in London, Ashby was only able to do a first cut before the film was taken to Europe. However, the producer of that film introduced him to Norman Jewison, and thus started a long and fruitful association between the filmmakers. Ashby edited The *Cincinnati Kid*, *The Russians Are Coming, the Russians Are Coming*, *In The Heat of the Night* (for which he won an Oscar), *The Thomas Crown Affair*, and *Gaily, Gaily* for Jewison.

Jewison also promoted Ashby to associate producer status, and when he had problems scheduling *The Landlord* (1970), Ashby was given the opportunity to direct, thus fulfilling that seemingly impossible dream he had fifteen years ago. But now he had arrived and there would be no stopping him. He followed his initial critical success with *Harold and Maude* (1971), *The Last Detail* (1973), *Shampoo* (1975), and *Bound for Glory* (1976).

Ralph Appelbaum: Why has there been a reluctance on the part of Hollywood to deal with the Vietnam issue?

Hal Ashby: That's a question that has been asked by almost everybody who has seen the film, and I wish I could answer it. I directed my first film in 1969, and at that time—even the two or three years before that—I cannot recall any serious conversation by individuals contemplating such a project, which is not something I'm particularly proud of, because I never instigated it either. But, understand, the possibility of a film about Vietnam was never thrown at me. Another interesting question is why have they suddenly begun to explore that area, because in addition to our film, there are a number of others coming out. Maybe Hollywood is bothered by their conscience, maybe they feel they sidestepped it. It's a very interesting question and I wish I could give a definite answer as to why. I mean, I even asked myself the same question when I decided to do the film.

Appelbaum: I believe that the only film to deal with Vietnam in the 1960s was John Wayne's *The Green Berets*.

Ashby: That's right. Listen, we had one critic refer to this picture as the liberal *Green Berets*. Well, that's just what I had in mind (laughs). Can you imagine that, all of us sitting down and saying, "Now we're going to make a liberal *Green Berets*." I may make mistakes, but I'm not an idiot.

Appelbaum: Were you politically active during the war years?

Ashby: Yes. I was active in as many things as I was able to deal with, none of them being enough—you know, there was just the pressure of keeping the pressure on, and the frustration of knowing that nothing was enough. I marched around and said what I had to say. It's very interesting because Los Angeles, if for no other reason than the geography of it, is usually passive and not willing to get involved in causes. But there was a great deal of activity there in the '60s. For example, if Nixon, or others like him, came into town and stayed, say, at the Century Plaza, the people came down and they protested, they made their views known. People became united, they walked hand in hand with each other, and that was wonderful. In a sense, however, the only thing that was not so wonderful was the reason for this unity—and that was the war.

Appelbaum: When you agreed to direct the picture, what type of research did you do?

Ashby: Once I commit myself to a project, my main objective is to collect as much information as I can about the subject—even though much of it will be wasted and go down the tubes. In this instance, it meant spending time with the writer and reviewing whatever research he had done. I also hired a couple of research people. I even got my secretary and the girl I live with into the music of the '60s and I had them put every song that they could think of, and every song that I remembered fondly, on cassettes. They filled six of them.

Then I assembled the photographs I had collected and pinned them up on the wall of the room I do a lot of my work in. And to help me remember the period, I borrowed many films from the Vietnam Veterans Against the War, and I saw Frederick Wiseman's *Basic Training*. I just want to be like a sponge and absorb everything; that's my form of research. And at a certain point in doing this, I became very depressed (this usually happens just before or after I start shooting) because I realize that I'm only going to capture a small part of that period. You know, unless you're doing a documentary film, there are certain physical limitations that you must adhere to.

I think that doing a large amount of research gives you the edge, because if you've got that detail covered and are constantly working on it, those mistakes you make don't hurt as much. And I'm going to make mistakes I'll be unhappy with, to the extent that I will work on something else. But the research gives your film a base of reality and honesty. So that when those mistakes are made, you can look at them in a different way.

Appelbaum: *Coming Home* was five years in the development stages. Could you talk about its history and why three writers are credited with the screenplay?

Ashby: I think that Nancy Dowd was the first writer with Jane on the project. I never met her, and quite frankly I don't understand her having a screen credit, because her story was not used. I'm a stickler about credits. I don't like it when people use a contractual agreement to put their name on a film, especially when they've contributed nothing to a film. But, at the same time, I understand a lot of people contribute to the development of a project, and Dowd did work with Jane. However, I didn't know anything about her screenplay until six weeks into pre-production, when someone sent me another script by Nancy Dowd and mentioned that she did the original screenplay on this. I just answered, "Oh, really." And I asked Jerome Hellman, the producer, about it and he said, "Oh, yes, there was something done." And I said, "I've got to read that screenplay."

So I read her screenplay, which was called *Buffalo Soldiers*, to see if I could use anything from it. And I can't begin to tell you what it was about. It took place somewhere in Wyoming, and the woman was married to a sergeant who went to Vietnam and came back as a paraplegic. There was nothing in it that bore any resemblance to the structure Waldo had. And when I asked him about it, Waldo said he didn't care for that screenplay, but liked Jane's concept so much that he asked to do an outline. It was that sixty-five-page outline, which took him about six or seven months to write, that convinced United Artists to finance a screenplay; then when that was completed, they gave the go ahead to find a director.

Before I became involved, John Schlesinger had backed out of the project, and so I called him to ask why. Did they just decide they didn't want him? And he said something funny. He said, "It's so American that I don't think I could do it." I said, "Well, John, you do pretty good films about Americans." What he meant, he said, was that the Vietnam subject was so American, he didn't want the film opened to the kind of criticism where somebody could say, "What right has he to do it?" And in one sense, I understand his feelings about that. But if I was in that situation and the question came up, I would say that I have the right simply because it's there. But John felt strongly about that and he recommended they give it to me.

Waldo had done what I consider breaking the back of the story. Now, I don't know how close it was to Jane's ideas, but it had the feeling of what I wanted. He had this woman married to a Marine captain who was going to Vietnam during the Tet Offensive. And while he was away she goes to work as a volunteer in a hospital, meets this paraplegic, there is a love affair, and the husband comes home. But that concept changed a tremendous amount because I felt Waldo's script had too much rhetoric in it. I felt quite strongly that these should not be articulate people; maybe they really couldn't find the words to say what they were feeling. And as we were working on the screenplay, Waldo had a slight heart attack which limited his working time, and we had to start at a certain date because Jane was committed to do Pakula's film, *Comes a Horseman*, which was already put off for about a month and a half so we could slot this one in.

I remember that just before we started shooting, Jane said to me, "Have you ever started a film knowing no more about what we're going to do than this?" And I said, "No." She looked at me and said, "I hope it works." I said, "So do I." But I felt that because we were dealing with personal relationships in the film, the very fact that we were in limbo in certain areas would enhance it—we would be able to get deeper into the characters by not having the scenes worked out in advance; we might even discover things we wouldn't normally look for. So I felt pretty good about that, even though I knew it was going to be hard. There's enough problems in making a film without having to take that load and put it on top of everything else.

During the first two weeks of shooting, I had Rudy Wurlitzer, who's a writer, working on the screenplay. I could come home at eleven at night and we would work until about two in the morning. I don't know what material I used or didn't use from what Rudy wrote, but just the fact that he was from outside the production helped me a great deal. I had a big problem with the actors because they would say, "When are we going to get some pages?" And I would say, "I'm going to give you a whole bunch in about ten days or two weeks." But it really ended up, "What are we going to do for tomorrow?" or, even, sometimes, "What are we going to do today?" But like I said, I think overall it helped give the film that sense of reality and honesty.

The one place where the picture stretches the melodrama is, obviously, towards the end, when the three characters confront each other in the same room. I felt that even though we were pushing the melodrama, it was necessary to get those people together. People don't confront their responsibilities when it comes to dealing with others, and I wanted to put that on the screen, because that's what people should do, no matter how painful it is or how scared they are. Voight said, "I'd never do that, and this character would never do it." I said, "I know, Jon, but we're going to do it because that's what he should do."

Appelbaum: It's very risky to put Bruce Dern in a room with a loaded gun because it leads one to believe that . . .

Ashby: Somebody's going to get killed. Absolutely. But I'll tell you a story: I've known Bruce for a long time, and while I knew he's totally opposite from his screen image—he's a very gentle, kind, sweet man—I never knew he abhorred guns. We were in Hong Kong shooting the gunnery range scene, with Dern shooting the targets, etc., and you couldn't talk to him that day. All he said was, "I hate guns." It's funny because I thought Bruce knew all there was to know about guns. But I ended up showing him things. Mind you, I don't own any guns and never have. But my father collected them and so I learned how to use them. It wasn't until I watched some guys kill a deer that I decided it wasn't for me.

If there's one thing I do regret—and I don't really regret it—but it would have been interesting if we could have structured the Marine captain's part more evenly or given him more screen time, so that we would have learned more about him. I liked what Bruce was doing with the role—obviously, it was the more difficult one, and I felt he brought humanity to this character.

Appelbaum: I understand that Voight was originally set to play the Marine captain's role?

Ashby: Here's what happened with that: I have a very close relationship with Jack Nicholson, both as an actor and friend, and it would be very hard for me to imagine any male role that he couldn't do. So I thought he would be right for the paraplegic, and I spoke with him about it. I don't really try to sell him, I just say, "Jack, here's what I've got, would you be interested?" Then, I thought about Bruce or Jon for the other role—and I chose in my mind to give it to Jon first; just how I arrived at that I don't remember. The very next day Jon came to me and said, "Believe me, I will do anything in this picture. I would be glad to play the captain, but I would prefer Luke." And I spoke with Jon about it (we didn't know each other very well and he was nervous about being with me) and said, "That's interesting. Let me think about it for a bit. But you can be sure that I'll have a role for you."

Now, I went back to thinking about Bruce more strongly. This is one of the things I hate about casting, because you're dealing with people and not two blocks of wood. But when Jack couldn't do it because of prior commitments, all my problems were solved, and I gave the part of Luke to Jon and that of the captain to Bruce.

During the debating period in my mind of whether he was going to play the captain or not, Jon met a Marine captain in a coffee shop and he asked him (this was on tape) what he would do if he came home from Vietnam and found out his wife was having an affair with a paraplegic. He said, "I'd kill both of them. I'd kill her first because he's in a chair and wouldn't be as dangerous." And all this, mind you, was before Jon even got the role. But as soon as Jon knew he was going to play the part of the paraplegic, we got him a wheelchair and he practically lived in it. He went out and met different paraplegics. He played basketball with them, and they took to him right away.

Appelbaum: Did you use actual paraplegics in the film?

Ashby: Yeah. The only actors playing paraplegics were Jon and the guy with the ventriloquist's dummy. All the rest were para and quads. Every one of them; not an actor in the bunch.

Appelbaum: What comes through in the film is the attitude that these people are no different than any of us.

Ashby: Absolutely. In fact, they're actually more up than we are. No matter what their accident was, when they found out they were paralyzed for the rest of their lives, they got into some very heavy thoughts about ending it. But once they've made the decision to go on living, they become very positive thinking people.

Normally, during the course of making a film, people start moaning and groaning, because of the time it takes to set up a shot. But these people were very patient; not once did they complain. It's one of the only times that I can think of where I've been around fifty or sixty people for six weeks at a time and liked every one of them.

I felt very obligated to treat them full out as people—and that's why I don't show them complaining about their handicap. I think the only time Jon talks about being in a chair is in front of Jane's house that one night where he says, "When I dream I still see myself walking." I felt we had to touch upon the dreams that these people have.

Appelbaum: Going back to the screenplay: Could you give an example of a scene which worked better because it was loosely structured?

Ashby: There were so many. I would say that one was probably the confrontation scene, where the three of them meet in the room. That was never even written. What we did during rehearsal, a couple of weeks before we were going to shoot, was set up a tape recorder and have them improvise the scene from beginning to end for about four hours. Then I had that transcribed, and Bobby Jones, the writer, and myself constructed the scene from that material. They were just full of ideas.

Appelbaum: I understand Salt's script had an altogether different ending.

Ashby: At the end of his script, the Dern character, the captain, flashed-back to Vietnam and ended up holding hostages; then, when the police and helicopters came, he flashed-back even further and ended up getting killed on the freeway. He almost got talked out of it by Luke. And that was it. The end actually came a little later when Luke and Sally got back together after the funeral. It just didn't make it for me.

Appelbaum: Your ending has been criticized because it has the captain commit suicide by drowning himself.

Ashby: I know. But none of them has said very clearly what they didn't like. I thought it was pretty interesting—and it moved me a lot.

I didn't think it was too pat. I didn't say that Luke and Sally would definitely get back together. All I was trying to say was that this Marine wasn't strong enough to handle it. And that's pretty honest, I think. I'm not saying that every Marine captain couldn't handle it, but that this particular one couldn't.

Appelbaum: It seems to be that maybe they were looking for a happy ending where everything would be resolved. But that doesn't happen in every day life.

Ashby: Right. The last line in Waldo's script was a line I loved. I think Luke said, "You know, fuck this being alone shit," and they walked into the house together. But I couldn't bring myself to do that because I felt, Jesus Christ, first they have an affair while her husband is in Vietnam, and now, fortunately, he gets himself killed and they can be together. I didn't want the story to go that way.

Appelbaum: Did you have any problems with Fonda because she launched the project?

Ashby: No. We had no more problems on this than any other film where somebody says, "I don't know if this is going to work." Never once did she say that this was her idea. We never got into anything like that at all. We did get into many disagreements, but they had to do only with what we would be doing at a given time.

Appelbaum: Such as?

Ashby: There were different things that would crop up where somebody would say, "I just don't think this woman would do that." But most of that dealt with real small problems. For example, there was a scene when the captain brings his Marine buddies home, they tell jokes, get drunk, and as we pan around the room later that evening, we see her tearing a "Welcome Home" sign down. Well, the place looked too messy for her. She said, "I think that if this place was so messy, Sally would just be furious about it." So we cleaned it up a bit. That was the type of disagreements we had. I never saw her balk at doing anything.

Appelbaum: Was there a reluctance on her part to do the nude scene with Voight?

Ashby: She was concerned about it; about her image and what people might say. In other words, she felt that people would say, "I always knew that's what she did running along with the Black Panthers like she must have . . ." But she didn't do that, and I understood her feelings. I explained to her that those people were going to say it regardless of what's on the screen. As a matter of fact, my attitude was: if they come to a Jane Fonda movie at all it would be fortunate. She's outspoken but still basically a shy person. So we had that to worry about.

Appelbaum: *Barbarella* was just re-released to theatres because of the renewed interest in science-fiction films, and it's remarkable how she's grown as a person and performer since that picture.

Ashby: Yes, it really is. She's a remarkable person. She has so much energy that she can be thinking about twenty things at the same time, whereas maybe I'm down to my last one. And she can give equal time to each.

She has also maintained her career throughout the years. Usually, when someone becomes politically active and controversial, their popularity drops—even if they've won an Academy Award. But that never happened to Jane. I don't think I ever heard anyone say she would be too controversial for a role. And in Hollywood they are outspoken about matters such as that.

Appelbaum: There is almost a continuous flow of '60s music in the picture. Was this something you intended to do from the beginning?

Ashby: Well, I always knew I wanted to use music from that period, but I wasn't quite sure how I was going to do it. And when I got into the editing of the picture, I got a lot of questions about that from people who are into doing films in a conventional manner. I will say that if we had the money it would have been wall to wall music. I would have started it right over the UA logo and maybe even put a good disc-jockey in there now and then, like it was one big radio station playing. But I did the next best thing, which was to put in as many songs as I could. I concentrated on where they started rather than where they stopped.

And that had to do with a number of thoughts I had, the first one being that music was very important during the '60s, and if there was anything that could set that period better than almost any image that I could put on the screen, it would be the music. The other reason is that I believe people drift when they watch films. They may watch a certain scene and be so taken in by it that they are halfway into the next scene before they realize it. And I think that's a very natural thing to do. I certainly do it, and I'm certain a lot of others do too. So I felt that if they're going to drift, let them drift off into something that they did in their own life. Let them hear something and say, "Wow, that really takes me back to a certain place." Then they can come back into the flow of the picture. They're not really going to miss that much.

The ultimate hope, of course, is that if they enjoyed it so much, they'll come back for the parts they missed. Unfortunately, the cost of seeing a movie makes that prospect unlikely. I love the format of film, but it would be great if they could buy the film on a record or disc and play it on a console at home five, six, twenty, or a hundred times. And maybe you become so addicted to one sequence that you play it over and over again. Nothing would be more exciting than that, and it gives people a chance to see all the things you tried to do in the film.

Appelbaum: Your last film *Bound for Glory*, was a critical success but financial disaster. Do you think that one of the reasons for this could have been the casting of David Carradine as Woody Guthrie?

Ashby: I would hope it wasn't, because I think he did a fine job in it. And if that were the case, it would mean that audiences prejudged it, which I guess happens all the time. But I think it's more of a question of timing, where if a film came out a year or two earlier or even later than it did, it would have a better shot at making it—provided it's a good film to begin with. I don't know how to answer it except to say that it has to do with the mood people are in and what their interests are, etc. What I try to do with my films is not be too heavy-handed with them. And sometimes I think that has a lot to do with it, because if you are heavy-handed you sometimes stand a little better chance of grabbing an audience. But I don't want that to ever be my guide.

Appelbaum: Why did you choose Carradine for the part?

Ashby: When I started the film, I said, "I just want to think of Woody as an interesting character. I don't want to get into his physical look, and so forth." But after two weeks of research, I felt the actor had to look like Woody: he's got to be short and have that hair, etc. So I went through a whole period with that. In the meantime, I was meeting actors and recording artists. My casting director said that David's manager, a man I had known for many years, called and said David really wanted to talk with me about doing the Woody Guthrie role. I knew he was a good actor because of what I had seen, but I heard he was bad to work with, that he was irresponsible, and that he was morose. But I thought it was someone who might be putting a lot of thought to how Woody should be played, so I set up a meeting. David didn't, however, come in that way. He brought his guitar in, he sang his own songs, he never sang a Woody Guthrie song. But we spoke, and in the end what he was saying wasn't so much that he studied Woody Guthrie and felt he could play him, as it was people he knew had told him for years that he should play Woody Guthrie. And the more I got involved with what the spirit of Woody Guthrie was, which was his family and beliefs, the more David came closer to that than anybody else I met with. I got resistance along the way from people because of David, because of the *Kung-Fu* television show and all the adverse publicity surrounding him. When I met him, he was a man who had been living with Barbara Hershey for seven years, they had a baby, and they had broken up. So of course he was morose.

About six weeks later I brought him back in and put him on tape. I used an Advent, one of those four-feet-by-six-feet video screens, which are terrific for filmmakers as far as casting, because you can put people on them without pressure on yourself or the actor, and you can see them in close-up or whatever other angles you choose. So I put David on it so that other people could take a look and get as turned on as I was about the idea of him doing it. You see, I think he has a lot of charm. He has a neat smile. You talk to them about his smile and they look at you like you were crazy, like the man never smiled.

Appelbaum: Didn't you also speak to Arlo Guthrie, Woody's son, about doing the part?

Ashby: Yes. He was the first person I talked to, and he was interested in doing the part. But in the end I really felt that it would be too much of a load to ask somebody to play their father in a film. As far as I knew, he loved his dad very much and might have been able to play the role. But I felt that was a little risky, not just for the picture's sake, but for Arlo's as well.

Appelbaum: And UA didn't interfere with the casting?

Ashby: No. UA is exceptionally good for a film-maker in my estimation because they really do make it clear that it's up to you. I asked their opinion because I do want to keep them enthused about the picture, and in the end they're the ones who have to sell it. But it was made very clear to me that I didn't have to ask them anything. It was the same on *Coming Home*. Of course, they would have liked a bigger name than Voight for the role, but when I told them I was adamant about having him, they agreed and let me make the picture.

Appelbaum: Why did you decide to focus only on Guthrie's early life in the picture?

Ashby: I just felt that to cover his entire life would make the film less good. It took us two hours and twenty-seven minutes to cover what we did; any more than that would be another picture.

Appelbaum: How extensive was your research?

Ashby: Again, I put a lot of photographs from that period on my wall—photographs by Walker Evans and others. And, of course, there was a tremendous amount of other material on migrants available. We used the original research books from 20th-Century Fox's *The Grapes of Wrath*, which told of that particular period when migrants came to California. That incident we show in the film when the Los Angeles Police set up barricades two or three hundred miles away from the border to keep people out of the state of California was not, to the best of my knowledge, in any of Woody's writing, except maybe a song. It came out of the research we did.

Appelbaum: Was it difficult to re-create that period because of modern-day conveniences, such as TV antennas and telephone poles, etc.?

Ashby: Enormous. We kept on looking and looking for locations. And my production designer, Michael Haller, who's normally a very calm human being, became agitated. I don't know how many thousands of miles he drove—and he had other things to do. I told Michael very early on that I didn't want to make any high shots looking down at the ground. That's what everyone does on a period picture because you can cut out a lot. I wanted everything to be at eye-level. And it's difficult to say, "Let's go outside and start shooting 1937."

Appelbaum: Did you have to build any sets?

Ashby: We built the interior of the radio station. Originally, we had found a great old radio station in LA (I think it was KLA) that had been around since the '30s, and now the owners were moving it; they had bought a new building. And so we had the interior, the exterior, everything was terrific. But while we were up in Stockton, California, shooting, the Korean Press bought the building, and by the time we got back to LA to shoot there they had the presses all set up. So it was a location we lost. But I didn't regret that because we were able to rent a lot of their old equipment, and any time you build a set you're able to shoot freer. You can move walls and the crew around. You're much more relaxed.

Applebaum: How does your background as an editor affect the way you shoot?

Ashby: It doesn't affect it other than just knowing basically what pieces of film will cut together and what the composition should be. It's very important that the singles, or the over-the-shoulder masters, be basically the same size, because if something throws you off, you're limited by the amount of coverage you got. So, as a general rule, you have to be very careful about that. Most cameramen will pick that up—that's why they're always to the actor. But as far as pre-cutting the film in my head, I never have. I always shoot more film than I'll ever need. I prefer to edit that way.

Applebaum: But when you shoot more footage, isn't the film hurt as far as expositions and character development go?

Ashby: In my mind it doesn't hurt the film. I would rather be frustrated by having too much material than not enough. There's obviously many, many times when I say, "My God, why did I shoot that?" I mean, everything was working very good and I didn't need any more material. But I'm just going to let it ride along. I don't even question that. You just go with what you think is best.

Applebaum: I understand that for *Bound for Glory* you originally cut a shorter version and when UA saw it they asked that certain footage be put back in.

Ashby: When I first showed the picture to UA it was three hours long, and they genuinely liked the film and were moved by it. Now, when it came down to my end process, my assumption was that they would want a shorter running time so that the theatres would be able to get more screenings in. And it also said in my contract that I would deliver a two-hour picture. I don't pay much attention to those things, but I let them have it because it doesn't really have to do with anything real. However, I did think that they would want a shorter running time on the film. So I ended up with a version that worked very well and ran two hours and fifteen minutes. But when Arthur Krim and Pleskow saw the film again they talked about scenes they missed, scenes that emotionally affected them. They were scenes that I liked, but I never expected them to want the film made longer. So I re-investigated it and changed around the beginning of the picture. But UA made it very clear that if I was satisfied with the shorter version, it was fine with them.

In the shorter version, the opening scene was the square dance and dust storm. I put back into the picture the scene where Woody Guthrie comes into the gas station and they sit around and one guy comes up with the cards—the fortune-telling scene. That scene was originally out. He just came up to the gas station and sat around with the guys and said, "You folks sure are depressing." Another scene I put back in was when he got the lady to drink the water. A scene that was questionable, but I put it back in anyway, was when Randy Quaid comes to the radio station and talks about standing up for his rights. I've never been quite sure about that. Randy's a good actor and he does the scene wonderfully but it just upsets me.

Appelbaum: How hard do you work to visualize on film what's written in the script?

Ashby: Once, when I was working as an assistant editor on a film, George Stevens came up to me and said, "In film, 25 percent of it is in the writing, 25 percent of it is in the shooting, 25 percent of it is in the editing, and the last 25 percent is what you end up with." Making a movie is an horrendous undertaking. You can't lock yourself into anything. It's an ongoing process from the time I say I will do a film until the time I hand the distributor the cut film. The danger to me is if you fight so hard to put it down exactly the way you visualize it, and I've seen this happen, you bend it and bend it into something it isn't anymore, just because you've got something about it in your mind. If a scene vaguely represents what I had in mind, I'm happy as hell. The more latitude you give yourself, the better your chances for a good film. It's very personal, and I don't know how anyone feels about this other than myself.

Appelbaum: Is it true that on *The Landlord* you had problems with the Mirisch Corporation, the financiers of the film, because they felt the rushes were a bit on the dark side?

Ashby: Well, I think it must have been Walter Mirisch who actually flew in from the Coast, and we looked at the film, and he said, "It's too dark." And other people said, "You can't see their eyes." What I was trying to do was stylize a certain design, and I told them they must have faith in me. I said, "I'm not going along with the school of thought that because people laugh, you have to see their eyes real clear." People could stand in a dark hallway and say a funny line and laugh just as hard as you can if you've got a light turned on and you see them very clearly. I felt very strongly about that, and I wanted the whole ghetto part to have that ash look and Long Island to have that white look. I said, "I understand your plea, but that's what we're going for." I told my editor that on the next picture what we should do is just put up black leader and clear leader for dailies and tell them to have faith in me, that I have a design here (laughs).

Appelbaum: *Shampoo* is thus far your most successful film at the box-office. Could you talk about its genesis?

Ashby: Warren and I were just becoming friends and during dinner one night we talked about different ideas and he asked me if he had ever mentioned *Hair*, which was *Shampoo*'s original title. He didn't call it *Hair*; he just described the story. He said he and Bob Towne had worked on it when they were doing *Bonnie and Clyde* and that when Towne had finally written the script and given it to him to read, he was so angry with it that he sat down the next day and wrote his own version. I read both versions, and I told him I thought it would make an interesting film because of the interactions between the characters. And he and I sat down and we took pages from each one just to get an overall idea. Then we got Towne to come in, and we sat for about, I guess, seventeen or eighteen days, almost twenty-four hours a day, in this hotel suite, trying to get a first draft of those two scripts together.

Appelbaum: When it came to the actual making of the film, was there any friction between you and Beatty?

Ashby: I was the director of the film and I had as much control as I have on any film. Beatty would exert a tremendous amount of influence on everybody because of what he felt about the film, and so forth. But everybody does that. And we had Towne around all the time. All I care about is what I'm seeing every day at the dailies. I don't care how we get it. I really liked working with Warren. There was never any power struggle on the film, because I would walk away from it in two seconds.

Appelbaum: *The Last Detail*, I'm told, was a problem film because of the explicit dialogue.

Ashby: Columbia Pictures, the distributor, said to me that they didn't want to totally emasculate the film, but they wanted my help in toning down the language. They felt the language was going to be offensive and would keep them from reaching a broader audience. I just said, "No. The word 'fuck' is used in this picture eighty times. Are you saying that if we cut it down to where it's used only forty times the film will reach a broader audience?" I said to the president of Columbia Pictures, "I don't even know what the hell you're talking about_ You do know that the first time 'fuck' is said there's going to be fifteen people who get up and leave the theatre." Well, I convinced them to preview the film in San Francisco, and when the audience liked the picture, they dropped the whole matter.

Appelbaum: Why do you think *Harold and Maude* has become such a cult classic?

Ashby: I think it's probably due to a number of things, the first being the kind of black humour that's in the film. I also think that a lot of it has to do with what Ruth Gordon says about life and love in the film. That's the impression I get with the feedback. It's not that she said such profound things in the film, as it is maybe the way she said them. And the spirit of the film makes people laugh. They have a good time with it.

Cinema Chat with Hal Ashby

Richard Fernandez/1978

From *Audience* 10.2, Summer 1978, pp. 25–27.

Biographies of Hal Ashby usually read like this: "He hitchhiked to Hollywood from Ogden, Utah, in the early 1950s. He first worked as a multilith operator in Universal's story department, and soon became fascinated by the filmmaking process."

I showed him that particular bio which United Artists had given me, and Ashby had a hearty laugh: "It always fascinates me how they compress years of pain and frustration into two sentences."

Before directing his first feature film, *The Landlord*, Ashby worked as editor on *The Big Country, The Loved One, In the Heat of the Night*, to name just a few. His films as a director, following *The Landlord* in 1970, are: *Harold and Maude, The Last Detail, Shampoo, Bound for Glory*, and his most recent, *Coming Home*, which stars Jane Fonda, Jon Voight, and Bruce Dern.

Ashby's next film will be *Hawkline Monster*, based on the Richard Brautigan book, which Ashby will be writing the script for; it will star Jack Nicholson.

The following interview took place while Ashby was in New York doing publicity for *Coming Home*.

Richard Fernandez: You were an editor for a good ten years before you directed your first feature. In all that time, did you ever try to get a film off the ground through independent financing?
Hal Ashby: That wasn't done as much when I was editing. The first job I worked on as an editor was for an independent movie. The filmmaker had raised $250,000 himself and then finally found someone to distribute the picture. But there were only a few people around Holly-

wood doing that. I don't think I was knowledgeable enough to go out on my own. I did try, but with no success.

RF: Norman Jewison is responsible for your start as director, isn't he?

HA: Right. I was pretty comfortable as an editor. I believed I was good at it, which gave me a secure feeling. So I sat back and really got into it, not thinking too far ahead about my future. It was Norman who asked me where I wanted to go and what I wanted to do with the rest of my life. I expressed interest in directing, and he said, "Let's find something for you to do."

RF: He found *The Landlord*.

HA: Yes. That was originally developed for Norman, but he was too busy doing other pictures. There was no way in the world I would turn down this chance to direct.

RF: And eight years later you're considered a "hot commodity." What does it mean to mean to be "hot"?

HA: I get to see a lot of material. But more importantly, it means that I can get made almost anything I choose.

RF: What about the saying that you're only as hot as your last film?

HA: I never believed that success had to do with whether or not your pictures made money, as much as it had to do with showing these business types that you know how to handle a camera, and that you *can* make a feature film—with some talent. Now, if all my films were dismal failures, then I'm sure I would have problems getting another one made.

RF: Was *Bound for Glory* the most time-consuming film you've done to date?

HA: It sure was, close to a year. I think my budget was a little over seven million dollars, too. Shooting the big crowd scenes and working in the trains was so fucking hard on me physically.

RF: Was the choice of David Carradine to play Woody Guthrie made early on, or were there a lot of actors considered?

HA: There were hundreds. Tim Buckley was one. Dustin Hoffman another. But Dustin wanted to take time off to learn to play the guitar. The hell with that. It was Warren Beatty who pointed out to me, while I was casting the film, that Carradine had the right "I don't give a fuck" attitude I was looking for. David captures Woody's spirit better than anyone could, I think.

RF: How did your involvement with *Coming Home* start?

HA: Through Jane Fonda, screenwriter Waldo Salt, and producer Jerome Hellman. There was a lot of work being done on the script, but that was all hearsay to me. Nancy Dowd, who wrote *Slap Shot*, was also involved in working up the script, which I didn't even know until eight weeks after joining on. John Schlesinger was Hellman's first choice as director, since they had worked together on two previous pictures. But then you had the problem of an Englishman doing a story about the Vietnam war. Schlesinger turned the project down.

RF: The approach to the story and your style of shooting were really quite simple and realistic. You didn't clobber us over the head with a heavy message.

HA: Absolutely not. Waldo's first draft had none of that. Our draft did add more protests—as when Jon Voight chains himself to the recruiting office fence. That particular scene was first written as a bunch of paraplegics taking over one of the administration buildings of the Veterans Hospital.

RF: That was a part of the period.

HA: It was, but it wouldn't have been right for our film. It would have been standard material. I thought, what personal thing can *this* guy do out of frustration? I knew I didn't have to verbalize too much about the paraplegics, they're as graphic as anything you want to see.

When I started shooting, I found the script to be a bit talky; but I felt if we really got into the characters' heads we'd pull off a good story.

RF: When the three people confronted each other, at the end of the film, I found I wasn't hating the Bruce Dern character, but feeling sorry for him.

HA: That's what I wanted. It's very easy to hate, isn't it? Here's a guy who's a stereotype Marine captain, someone we don't feel terribly friendly towards. I certainly don't spend *my* time with those types. There's no growth to them. There is, however, growth to Dern's character. I wanted to take a look at him and realize just how sad this man really is.

RF: This confrontation is the most melodramatic section of the film.

HA: No question about it. The original script called for Dern to hold hostages; later, Voight meets with him, talks him down, and Dern is subsequently killed on the freeway. But we've seen all that before, and Vietnam veterans already have such a heavy load to carry. I wanted those people to confront each other in a room, and *talk* about what has gone down.

RF: That scene raises the question—as does the entire film—of our responsibilities.

HA: That's such a big part of the film's meaning. These people had an affair while her husband was in Vietnam, which has a lot to do with his breakdown. But it wasn't just Vietnam—it was everything that built up inside him. Rarely do people kill themselves for just one reason. The film especially raises the question of responsibility to the veterans . . . and the responsibility to each other.

RF: Isn't there a bit of manipulation on your part, when they confront each other, by letting Dern have a gun?

HA: It was something I thought about heavily, and yes, I did manipulate the audience there—maybe a bit too much. Here was a man who not only lived with guns but, in that one scene, slept with them when he returned home. But all I was trying to show was that the Voight and Fonda characters did care about that other person. The ending has a feeling of being an epilogue, because of the melodramatic height. I had the option of ending the picture with just Voight coming down the walkway and stopping. I decided to go one step further—to show that Dern couldn't cope and that life goes on.

RF: I felt that Dern had a chance—?

HA: Did you? No, he's gone. He's completely out. I eliminated a couple of shots that had him *way* out in the water, when he went for the swim. There's little or no chance for him.

RF: Let me ask you about the radio music in the picture. It's almost nonstop.

HA: Exactly. I thought, while editing this film, that the music actually has more controversy than anything else. I was planning to hire a good FM dee-jay to come on at the beginning of the film and introduce a radio program which would last for the next two hours. I got some pretty strange looks from the people at United Artists. We didn't have the bread to go quite that far.

RF: In an effective way, the music definitely goes against the grain.

HA: But it fits, right? I wanted it on *all* the time—have these characters speaking dialogue while the radio or television is on. Isn't that what we do in life? Plus, I knew the music would make people reflect back to what they were doing in 1968.

RF: Letting them drift away for a while?

HA: That's what I wanted. They're not going to lose the flow of the film. *Let* the music take them somewhere.

RF: You've managed to make extremely personal—even offbeat—films that are starting to hit with a large audience. You're now working in the mainstream of the film industry. How do you view your standing in that industry?

HA: That's hard to analyze. I hope more films move towards personal cinema, because that is where I'm at. These big-budgeted, splashy movies will always be around, they have great appeal for many. The fact that a *Star Wars* or a *Close Encounters* can gross millions of dollars is very attractive to those who finance films. But I intend to keep making personal pictures.

RF: How can you maintain such a perspective and keep your values intact with all the bullshit around you in the industry?

HA: I don't know if I do it with any real conscious design. I've always led a very simple life. There are so many things that have molded my present set of values. The music I listen to, which is a big part of my life, for example . . . and any of the arts that put you in motion and make you think. Materially, I'm living very comfortably; I can afford the things I need. But it's not as if I've been striving for all this. It's just starting to happen now and it's all very weird for me. I just won't let it take me over . . . I won't lose that basic value.

RF: You seem to keep your career moving.

HA: Now *that* has been a conscious effort on my part. You know, I never believed I was not wanted in the industry. I feel as though people are starting to listen, and that as much as I can ask for. If it can happen for me, it can happen for Jerry Schatzberg, for Henry Jaglom, and certainly for John Cassavetes. I don't think I'll ever be totally happy, but I feel satisfied right now with what I'm able to do.

Dialogue on Film: Hal Ashby

James Powers/1980

From *American Film*, May 1980, pp. 53–60. © 1976 American Film Institute. Reprinted with permission of the American Film Institute.

Hal Ashby appears briefly—all of a few seconds—in his latest film, *Being There*. The setting is the editorial office of the *Washington Post*. Casually dressed, hair unkempt, Ashby is standing in the background, a *Post* employee languidly lost in work at a filing cabinet.

The cameo fits the style of the director. "He has such a light touch," Jack Nicholson once told an interviewer, "that some people who have worked with him aren't even sure he's directed the picture." That light touch—an open, nonrigid approach to filmmaking—has been applied during ten years as a director on such movies as *The Last Detail*, with Jack Nicholson; *Shampoo*, with Warren Beatty; *Coming Home*, with Jon Voight; and on the film that has become a cult favorite here and abroad, *Harold and Maude*, with Bud Cort and Ruth Gordon.

These films have established Ashby as one of Hollywood's leading— and more maverick—directors, free to pick and choose his scripts, free to select the actors he wants, free to go his own way. He is already booked for years to come, and a look at the Ashby films in the works shows the unpredictable range of his interests: "Lookin' To Get Out," a story about gamblers, with Jon Voight and Burt Young; "The Hawkline Monster," described as a "gothic Western" and based on the Richard Brautigan novel; and "Henderson the Rain King," based on the Saul Bellow novel set in Africa. Opening this year is his newest film, *Second Hand Hearts* (once *The Hamster of Happiness*), with Robert Blake and Barbara Harris. It's a romantic comedy set in Texas.

Ashby's own roots are in the West. He was born, during the Depression, in Utah, where his father ran a dairy. Ashby's rural upbringing found its way into *Bound for Glory*, his 1976 film about Woody Guth-

83

rie's wanderings in the Southwest. At seventeen, Ashby abandoned a job repairing railroad bridges and hitchhiked to California. He managed to get work at a film studio.

By the early fifties, Ashby was learning film editing. He worked on films like *The Loved One* and *The Russians Are Coming, The Russians Are Coming*, and in 1968 won an Oscar for his editing of *In the Heat of the Night*, directed by Norman Jewison. It was Jewison who opened the way to a new career. Busy with other projects, Jewison offered Ashby *The Landlord*, and in 1970, nearing forty, Ashby made his debut as a director.

In the Dialogue, speaking with engaging informality, Ashby recalls his first days as a director. He also talks about *Being There* and *Coming Home*, his work with Peter Sellers and screenwriter Robert Towne, his open working style on the set and in the editing room, and he speaks his mind, as he typically does, about Hollywood bureaucracy.

Question: The ending of *Being There* has provoked a good deal of comment. Do you have a definitive answer when you're asked what the ending means?

Hal Ashby: It means whatever you want it to mean. That's basically it. I had another ending, which I shot. It worked very well. Shirley MacLaine goes after Peter Sellers when he leaves the funeral and goes into the woods. She finds him and says she was frightened and was looking for him. He says, "I was looking for you, too, Eve." And they just walk of together.

But I was working one Sunday with a writer by the name of Rudy Wurlitzer, who was really interested in the film, and we progressed in the afternoon to talking about it. I said that because of the way Peter was playing this film, I knew what we were going for was a childlike kind of thing. And when Rudy asked me how it was going, I said, "Rudy, the way it's going with these characters and what's happening with them, I could have this guy walking on water at the end of the film." Then I said, "Well, I think I *will* have him walking on water at the end of the film."

So that's what I did. One guy in the crew said, "You can't have him walking on water." I said, "Why?" He said, "Well, you know the only person that walks on water." I said, "Jesus, or maybe some other godlike figure?" He said, "Yes." And I said, "Well, what is wrong with childlike innocence being godlike?" You could break it down that way if you wanted to. Whatever—you could break it down for a good laugh.

Question: How did Peter Sellers prepare for the role of Chance?

Ashby: Peter likes to go for the voice first. If he can find what the voice is, then it's very easy for him to locate the person. He didn't know what to do with this one—"Where is this guy from?" So we talked about the different possibilities. It was very difficult, but it was something he had to struggle with himself. It's very difficult to do that childlike delivery of lines and not have them sound like bad readings.

Question: What sort of possibilities did you talk about?

Ashby: As I said, we talked a lot about the voice. I believe I told him to start with a little bit of what he had in *Lolita*, mixed with his own sound, because his own sound to the American ear is cultured—even though it isn't, it's just an English sound. The best way to describe Peter: When he finished this picture, he went to work on a picture called *The Fiendish Plot of Dr. Fu Manchu*. He was rewriting the script himself, and he called me from Europe one day and read me the first ten pages he had written. He did all the parts on the phone for me—even did FDR—and they were all incredible.

He's the fastest mimic I've ever seen in my life. If he meets you, I guarantee you in thirty seconds he can do you—he picks up characteristics and moves. It's unbelievable how fast he works.

Question: Was the character of the president, played by Jack Warden, direct from the script, or did you make additions?

Ashby: The lines are basically what we came out with in the script. It's just that Jack is such a unique actor. Jack's timing is totally spectacular and special, and the character takes on something that nobody else could possibly do. I had the idea one day of casting Jack for the president, and I just couldn't from that moment on think of anybody else as the president.

Question: One of the targets of *Being There* is television. Did you consider making more of a comment about it than you did?

Ashby: Well, for me it makes plenty of comment. I mean, you've got a guy sitting there watching television, and he mimics everything—that's his life, watching it. As far as making a statement of what television really does, the thing that comes out of it for me, very clearly, is the children's shows. They're very strong in the film, if you listen; all they do is talk about friends, about love and special people. And so it all makes its own comment on just what it is. It's what it is. It's what every individual does with it that counts. It can be the greatest tool in the world, and it can be the greatest detriment in the world.

Question: Did you have a good working relationship with Caleb Deschanel, the cinematographer of *Being There*?

Ashby: I've known him for years. I met him on *The Landlord*. He was a student at USC, and he came back to meet Gordy Willis. I always kept track of Caleb. The designer Mike Haller went to help him with a film he was doing in Valley Forge, and Mike told me he was in the union. Then he was up shooting *More American Graffiti* when I had just finished *Second Hand Hearts*. I called and said, "You've got to come and do the film." He's really incredible. I can't find the words to tell you what I think of him.

Question: Was he involved during preproduction in working on the look you wanted in *Being There*?

Ashby: Absolutely.

Question: How much time did he have before shooting started?

Ashby: I don't know how much I gave him. I finished shooting *Second Hand Hearts* in October 1978, and I started shooting *Being There* in January 1979, so he must have come on in November sometime. I remember we went around and spent a lot of time going over stuff together, so I think of it as quite a while. Caleb puts a lot of time in. He was still looking at prints after the opening.

Question: How did you get involved with your previous movie, *Coming Home*?

Ashby: I came into it when Waldo Salt's script was sent to me. John Schlesinger was supposed to do it. I called John to see why he wasn't in it any more. He said because it was too American. I said, "What are you talking about? You do good American films." He said, "No, the subject matter." In other words, what the hell right does an Englishman have to come and make a da-di-da-di-da. Whatever it was, I knew he obviously didn't want to do it. So I committed to do it.

When I told United Artists I wanted to cast Jon Voight, I remember Mike Medavoy sat there and said, "No way. Absolutely. The man has no sex appeal." He gave me a whole big line of reasons not to cast Jon Voight in the role. Unfortunately, I'd already made up my mind. That's the kind of resistance you run into—"You got this wrong," and so forth. Nonetheless, it moved ahead pretty well.

I had Waldo's script and Bob Jones's script. But as soon as I was two days into the shooting, I saw where Jon was coming from with his character, so I just threw the first script out. We wrote the script as we shot. That's the only time I've ever done that. That's hard. I got Rudy Wurlitzer to come in. I would come home at about eleven at night, and we'd work till about four in the morning, and I'd get to work at six. We just wrote all night. I knew we had to go ahead on it because I can stand to do that for only about ten days or two weeks. You just physically can't take it.

I told Rudy I wanted to find out where Jon was going with this character, what we were structuring, and what we were going toward. It had a lot to do with some of the conversations I'd had with Waldo Salt. I think we accomplished most of the ideas he described and wanted to go toward. From what we discussed, he would have liked to see the Bruce Dern character sign up again and go back to Nam. That would have been his suicide wish. I was very much in tune with that, but I didn't know how in the hell to do it after that much film. That's a lot of stuff to explain all of a sudden.

Question: How do you see the Dern character?

Ashby: He was a casualty, a walking casualty, just like Jon was a casualty. But Jon is the central character in that film because Jon is the one who comes up the strongest. Jon at the end is saying, "There is a choice to be made here." That's what the film is about—that's the strongest central character you can get for me.

Question: At the end of the film, the Dern character runs into the Pacific. There was another ending originally, wasn't there?

Ashby: The end of it was holding hostages, for Christ's sake, and then getting killed on a freeway. That was the end of the picture at one time. I just kept looking at that, and I said, "I know I saw that on television one night when I was flicking by all the channels. That's been done." So that evolved into a whole thing. I didn't know what ending I was going to shoot on the picture until four weeks before I was finished shooting the picture—I mean, I didn't know.

Question: Did that make the executives a little nervous?

Ashby: I don't even know if they knew. When I was doing that writing with Rudy, by the way, their input was: Oh, my God, you ought to do this with it, and you ought to do that. I came home one night, and I remember that Medavoy and others were all going to visit the set the next day. I noticed that there was some pink paper there. I read it, and it was some notes from some story editor in New York about the script.

But the first two goddamn paragraphs were about how I had miscast the film, how I'd made this horrible mistake—and it didn't matter what the hell I did with the screenplay, because it wouldn't work anyway. I thought about that one all night while we worked. In the morning I called up Jerry Hellman, the producer, and I said, "Just call Mike Medavoy's office and tell them if they come on the set, I go off the set."

Question: Did working on the script while you were shooting create something of an unstructured atmosphere on the set?

Ashby: Even though I'm that unstructured, I *am* structured. I mean, I would talk with the actors the night before and say, "Here's what I think we ought to do tomorrow," and give the reasons why I thought we should do it. And they'd all come in with their lines, and they were great. They were terrific. And that all was guided by Jon's character—I threw out a screenplay because of where he was. That man received incredible amounts of resistance—down to everybody, including Jane Fonda, wanting him to play it more macho. I remember Haskell Wexler at one point said to Jon, "Why don't you just reach out and grab her?" I said, "Because he's not going to reach out and grab her. Jon is too scared to reach out."

One thing we were all relating to were the guys in wheelchairs during the first six weeks we shot at a veterans hospital. There were about fifty people in chairs around all the time.

Question: They had volunteered to be in the film?

Ashby: Yes. They had decided they wanted to live. I never talked to one of them that I didn't hear that the most serious thing he went through was the time he didn't know if he wanted to live or not. They didn't talk about hope—they didn't *ever* talk about getting up and walking.

Question: You shot rap sessions with them, didn't you?

Ashby: Yes, just two cameras sitting around. I have a lot of good film. I have a whole lot of footage of these rap sessions—I must have sixty thousand feet. They talked about everything. They talked about when they first came home, they talked about their first date, they talked about their children. I want to make that available to someone. I have some other rap sessions which are really heavy. One that took place in Jon's apartment was really an incredible session—anyway, I go off on that. Let's talk about something else for a minute.

Question: Well, how about Bud Cort?

Ashby: Bud Cort?

Question: Yes. Was he your choice for *Harold and Maude*?

Ashby: Absolutely. Everybody that's in my pictures is my choice.
Question: Is it a look you go after—like your choice of Peter Sellers for
Being There?
Ashby: Well, with Bud, I met a lot of young people for the role in
Harold and Maude. But Bob Downey probably said it best after he'd seen
the picture. He said, "He's a bar of Camay with two eyes." That's not
exactly what I thought when I saw the picture—I mean, I didn't know
that's what I had in mind. In that case it is a look, but it was also what
Bud gave to it. It was a whole thing he brought to the picture.

With Peter, he gave me the novel *Being There* in 1973, and I read it,
but we just couldn't get the money to make the film then. After I'd just
finished *Coming Home* and was trying to make some kind of a new deal,
Andy Braunsberg walked in with it and asked if I'd be interested. That's
when Ryan O'Neal was suggested for the film. But I said there was no
way—just on the level that Peter gave me the book was enough, plus
that's who I saw in the role. To start with, you just don't do that to
people. If he had given me the book and I wasn't interested, that would
be something else again.
Question: How did you work with Ruth Gordon in *Harold and
Maude?*
Ashby: Ruth was great. She's just all that energy that you would imagine she is. She was seventy-five then, so she ought to be eighty-three or
eighty-four years old now. Every time I see her, she's still going strong.
One of the funniest things that ever happened on that film was when
I got Tom Skerritt as the motorcycle cop. Tom is a very loose actor, but
whatever he would say, Ruth would still say her lines. She was a stage
actor and those were her lines, and if those were the lines, that's where
she was going. She was everything about that role that should have
been there.
Question: You were once a film editor. What led to your directing your
first film, *The Landlord?*
Ashby: I was very fortunate in all that. I knew I was a good editor.
I almost settled in there, because I got a lot of gratification. I'd been
trained real good by Bob Swink, who just taught me everything. I always was very rebellious and I fought real hard. I remember the first
picture I ever cut for Norman Jewison. He asked me one day if I felt he
should come down to the cutting room, and I asked him why. He said,
"Well, I don't know. Maybe to help you pick some takes and things." I
said, "If you don't trust me, why don't you get somebody else? I'm go-

ing to cut this picture. Then we'll take a look at it and see how it looks."
That sort of stuff. I had that relationship with Norman.

Norman set the thing up for me in the end. He asked me one day,
"What do you want to do?" I said, "I want to direct. That's all I've ever
wanted to do." But I hadn't even talked to him about it. I'd been with
him for three pictures by that time. He said, "Well, let's find something
for you." About the time we were just finishing up the shooting on
Gaily, Gaily, he said, "How would you like to do *The Landlord?*" I said,
"You kidding?" The last few years, from *In the Heat of the Night* on, I was
like his assistant. I had a real close relationship with him. It was real
good of him in all ways. I mean, I got $2 million to make my first film,
I had a lot of help, I got to shoot sixty-five days.

Question: How did you handle the change from editing a film in a
little dark room to dealing with—

Ashby: With people? Well, there were two things I was really scared
about. One was how to communicate with the actors. On my first film,
I cast Beau Bridges, and I'd worked previously on a film with him. We
had become friends, so I felt comfortable. I had worked as associate
producer, not as an editor, on *Gaily, Gaily*, so I wasn't around the set a
lot, but I got to know Beau. I felt comfortable there, but I didn't really
know how to communicate with the other actors. I was terrified about
that aspect of it.

The other was just how much of me would come out on the film,
because I really feel strongly about film being a communal art. I really
encourage that from everybody—to try and get as much creativity as I
can from everybody that's working on the film. It took me about thirty
seconds of watching the film not to worry about how much of me was
going to be on the film, because it would be all me as much as it would
be everybody else. You don't do any film unless you want to make it, so
once you have a real reason to do it, it will always be you.

As far as with the actors, it took me about three days. The first day
I couldn't talk. I'd worked myself into a state of walking pneumonia
and was just gasping all day and pointing a lot. I wasn't working with
anybody but Beau, so it was easy. But it took me about three days to
find out that I could communicate with them, so I enjoyed it from that
point on.

Question: Do you find yourself now approaching a film with the editing process in mind?

Ashby: The only editing process I have in mind is how I think the shots are going to look, the juxtaposition of shots. As far as the editing itself, I don't have any preconceived thoughts about it at all. That's why I wanted to do two pictures back to back, so I could get even further away from any preconceived ideas. I don't think for me that's healthy. I like the spontaneity that goes on in film and work for it that way. I don't edit as I go along. I wouldn't do that to an editor, first of all. I mean, that's the thing I was talking about with Norman: After I've cut the picture, if you don't like it, then let's do something about it, but not before.

Question: Some directors like to be in the editing room when the film is first being cut. You don't?

Ashby: I would never go in the editing room. What I try to do is encourage any editor that I have working for me to take his first cut and really get into doing that first cut, because that's his shot—I mean, not that he's not going to contribute from that point on. When I edited *The Thomas Crown Affair* for Norman, I didn't go in the editing room until six weeks after he'd finished shooting. Now when I went in, I didn't leave it for seven months. I mean, I literally didn't leave it. I stayed in it, I slept in it, I lived in it for seven months. I worked that hard on it. I don't even know how many months it was after he'd finished shooting that he saw the thing.

I would give any editor who felt that strongly the same leeway. Unfortunately, not very many of them do. Most of them try to second-guess you. Most of them are interested in something else. I don't know what the hell it is. But Bobby Jones is the best editor I ever found.

Question: He's also writing?

Ashby: Yes. That's all he's doing now. I hired him as an editor on *The Last Detail*. I'd hired a young fellow to cut *The Last Detail*, but I looked at an hour and forty-five minutes of it, and I really almost got ill. I mean, I didn't know what the hell his point of view was at all, other than trying to use every piece of film I shot.

I don't have to see the film in the first cut. I couldn't tell you what film was in Donny Zimmerman's first cut of *Being There* and what we ended up with. I ended up at four in the morning the day we opened making the last change that I can remember. I was sitting in the cutting room all night because we were behind on the thing.

Working on two pictures was very good for me because one of the things you want to do is always to try and get your mind clear, first of all. When you do an editing process, it has a tendency to go by sequence. In other words, when you go in, you sit down and you have such and such a problem. You discuss it—a certain portion, a certain reel, a certain scene. Scene by scene usually—otherwise, I'd get up and walk away. I would do that so I wouldn't become too restless. I have a tendency when I get restless, because I physically know how, to say, "Let me do it."

By the way, I'm going to start editing everything on tape now. I'm going to get one of those great big goddamn Mach 1 tape editing things. I tell you, it's going to be great. I don't know if I'll save any time, but I'll sure explore a lot of ideas, and I can find out real quick if they work or not.

I think Kubrick started the whole system. The last I heard, Stanley claims he can find any line in any take in twenty seconds. He's got four-teen playback machines going. I'm just getting into the whole thing about computers and everything. I think it's incredible.

Question: But you're still going to let the editor edit first?

Ashby: Oh, absolutely. Mark Harris, who's been working as an assistant with me these past five years, has been taking a course. We're building all that goddamn stuff. He'll have to teach me how to work it. I may never be in the editing room again because I won't physically know how to do it.

The other thing, by the way, which I'm really excited about—all my dailies for *Being There* and the other film I'm working on, *Second Hand Hearts*, are on tape. Now I can turn that over to the AFI. Anybody that wants to sit down and edit my film on tape can edit it. And I'm going to do that on all my films now and make the tapes available to places like the AFI, UCLA, USC. That's a great experience. You can just go in there and do anything you want to do with it.

Question: You say you let the editor do the first cut. Don't you even involve yourself in going through the takes and picking this one or that one?

Ashby: No.

Question: You give the editor the whole reel and say, "Cut it"?

Ashby: Hell, yes. He's got to be a big boy. He's the one who looks at it. It's the fourth and fifth time you see it that you start seeing stuff you never saw before—the stuff happening with actors, things like that. That's his job. That's what he sits down and looks for. The film will tell you how to edit it. The film will tell you what to do in the end.

The editor's the one who sits there the first time and investigates the film. I investigate it later—I can tell you. The last week before we opened *Being There*, I bet you I put fifty new pieces of film in that picture that had never been in the picture before. Now that's part of the process, too. I'm searching stuff out, just pursuing different ideas.

Question: But when you're looking at the film all cut together, how do you manage to remember that you have another take with a slightly different reading?

Ashby: By how it moves you.

Question: Let's back up a little. When you're still shooting a film, how far in advance do you plan a shot—or do you just go in and wing it?

Ashby: I just go in there and wing it—I'm lucky to get there in the morning. It's because of the structure of what goes on with the film. Let's say we're going to shoot a scene in this room. I've looked at the room before. I've got an idea of the area of the room that looks the best—that's what you basically want to go for when you're finding locations: what on the overall is going to look the best on film. But once you start walking around and looking, you see something else and you say, "Well, gee, that's interesting."

Then you bring the actors in—maybe the night before—and you say, "Why don't you sit down over there, and then we'll see what happens." Then you start working it down to where you got it pretty much in line with what you're thinking about.

Question: Is it just you and the actors at these early rehearsals, or is the cameraman there, too?

Ashby: I usually have myself and the cameraman and the sound man on those first rehearsals—plus anybody else who wants to stand around and watch. They're all going to go to work on it. As many people that can watch what's going on, the more information they have—you know, instead of just all of a sudden being out there in the dark.

It all depends on what the scene is, how intimate the scene is, but I basically want the actors to work it out in some free form. I don't want to come in and make them fit the camera. I would rather make the camera fit the actors. Let that be our job. We're skilled.

Question: What happens next?

Ashby: Now we've got the thing worked through. It's going to take three or four hours to light it, so during that time the actors can be working on lines. Then we bring them back in, and we rehearse it again to do it with the finer lighting, which is another half hour. But none of the pattern is going to change. Out of the whole thing, maybe an hour is different than what it would be if you had walked around and said, "Well, this is it."

Now if you really want to work fast, then you go in the night before, and you say, "OK. We're going to put the camera here, Caleb, and light this way, and so forth. The actor will be here and then will be there." And when the actors come in in the morning, you say, "OK. That's where you go and that's where you go." They say, "Well, gee, I kind of felt like maybe I ought to come through the door." You say, "No, no. No door." So you spoil even the possibility because you're locked into it, and you stop exploration of film. Always do as much exploration as you can. You'll never regret it.

Question: So during the first blocking of a scene, you're working just with the actors, instead of with the crew, too.

Ashby: I just have the crew around to watch, so they are all familiar with what's going on. There are fifty people in that crew, and in the end almost all of them are directly related to what is going on with the actors and what we're photographing. Whether it's the grips or the gaffers or whoever the hell it is, they all have to know what you're shooting for. Once you get that kind of cohesion working for you, all that crew stuff works great.

Big crews are great, by the way, when they're good. It's incredible, watching those guys work. In Ben's bedroom in *Being There*, we had the lighting from out the window. So we had a scaffold built that was four stories high, and that's the windy side of that house. Once in a while I'd peek out there. I watched these guys stand out there with those goddamn arcs, four stories up in the air with the wind blowing against them, holding those lights in the freezing cold. They're there all the time—those guys are there.

Question: You make use of a lot of rock music in *Coming Home*—and in *Shampoo*, too. How did that come about?

Ashby: Well, I'm just very locked in to music. When I got down to *Coming Home*, I knew I wanted the music. It takes you somewhere—I mean, it's good for the film because it puts you in a different time period than what you're actually sitting in. All I wanted to do was take people to wherever they would go. There are going to be a couple of songs that are going to do something to them. They can drift out of the film for a while, if they want to. All I listened to from the time I started shooting the picture until I finished that picture were cassettes.

Question: Did you have a lot of the songs already in mind for *Coming Home?*

Ashby: Oh, no, no. Right on down through the editing process I was changing songs all the time. The Rolling Stones play a big part because I'd been hanging out with Mick Jagger a little bit and listening to more music that way. Almost any goddamn thing in the picture, if we put a Stones song down to it, would just click—the way the rhythm of the film was going in relation to what was going with that music.

The music plays a big part in any of my films. I had it happen as an editor on *In the Heat of the Night.* I'd just gotten a Ray Charles album and was listening to it. He had a song called "Chitlins and Candied Yams." Haskell Wexler had been out with his assistant shooting the main title footage of the trains, and Haskell did a lot of stuff where he moves way out of focus. Now any time I've ever had silent footage, I've always put music with it. It's just crazy to sit there and watch an hour of silent film.

So I just laid the song in, and I'm telling you, the changes in music that went on were the changes that went on with the focus. I really started to realize the whole thing. I've always gotten into music in relation to film and what it does—just the rhythms that you have in the film at any given time and how they feed off the music.

Question: You did two with Robert Towne, the screenwriter—*The Last Detail* and *Shampoo*. What sort of relationship did you have with him?

Ashby: I don't know a writer that's as good as Bob in town. I don't know anybody that even comes close to him. He's in a whole other league. He's got a script he's going to start directing now which is incredible. It's about women athletes, called *Personal Best.* Boy, is it good. I told him, "I don't even know how in the hell you got inside those people." He said, "I don't either." It's the best thing I've read about women athletes and what goes on there. He's also going to do *Greystoke*, the Tarzan film, but he got so complicated into the damn ape systems. He's right—the ape outfits have to be one thousand percent believable.

By the way, in 1972, when Robert and I went to Catalina Island for ten days to work on *The Last Detail*, he first talked to me about doing *Greystoke*. Now it's eight years later, and he still hasn't done it—he hasn't finished the screenplay totally yet, as a matter of fact.

In between we did *Shampoo*, and he did help on a couple of other things. He was going to write *Personal Best* for me. I had told him, "You should do something in between because the Tarzan picture is going to eat you up." He said, "I have this thing I want to do about women athletes." Soon he had thirty pages. Once he got into it, I said, "Why don't you go ahead and do it? It will be a good first film for you to direct. I'm not going to do it." It's going to be great—the stuff reads right, feels right, comes to life.

Question: When you came in on *Shampoo*, had Towne already finished his script?

Ashby: Originally it was titled *Hair*. That's how long ago it was written. When I came into it, Warren Beatty sat down with me and told me the whole story of Bob taking a year and a half to write the screenplay and Warren being so angry by the time he got it that he sat down the next day and started to write his own version. So I sat there and read both versions. Then I said, "I think it's a really terrific film for us to do, but let's just you and me spend four or five days going through the two scripts and compiling the feelings of the scripts, the sense of the characters. Then once we've done that, let's give that to Bob and then ask him to come back." We actually all worked together on that.

Question: I've read what I guess is Towne's original script of *Shampoo*, but I found no descriptions of the characters or of places.

Ashby: It comes to life better than the reading of it. I prefer to be much looser with a script and pick up things as I go along. That has to do with my own thing about spontaneity in film. Not describing what the characters look like is always better. I never get any lock-in on what people look like when I'm reading a script. Scripts are hard to read. Most people don't know how to read them. They just don't know what they're trying to get out of them.

Question: How do you read them?

Ashby: I read them in general just to see what the idea is, to start with—what the hell kind of story we're trying to tell and why. I look to see what the rhythms are, and I try to hear certain things which give me an idea of how it starts to come to life. From that point on, it depends upon how good the writer is. That's why Bob Towne reaches the point where the stuff becomes magic. It comes to life very easy off the page with Bob.

Question: Do you worry about staying on schedule when you're shooting, or do you assume the money will come through if you run over?

Ashby: I fight real hard on the budget aspect—to where I've said I won't shoot the picture. I'm down to the point where I can really gauge it quite well just by habit. I know I'll shoot somewhere around seventy days—that's about what it takes me to shoot a film. The only one that was really different was *Bound for Glory*. We just got into train stuff on that. We got into stuff that physically was more than I'd ever dealt with before. The train comes down heading the wrong way, and you say, "Well, let's turn it around." They say, "Well, OK. It will take about twelve hours to turn the goddamn train around." They're not kidding either.

But I always assume they'll come up with the money. I never think they won't. You really have to be doing something wrong for them not to come up with it, because we all work real hard. The only time anybody sits around is when I don't have an idea. And sometimes I don't. Sometimes I don't know what the hell I want to do with a scene. Once in a while that happens, and we all sit around—or play a little football.

The big thing is to see that what you shoot can at least be put on film. That's what you fight hard for, and nobody fights harder for that than me. Those guys back in the production offices don't have a clue of what goes on in my heart, in my head, and what I'm thinking about. They don't know. They sit back there and they say, "Well, if he shoots tonight, that's going to cost $20,000." So what! Lorimar sent out memos on that kind of thing. Now none to me, believe me, because I get crazy when I hear that kind of stuff, and when you're shooting and you get crazy, they really get nervous.

Question: Do you draw the line on how expensive a project you'll get involved in?

Ashby: I think I would, just because of the way I function and the way I think. The whole inflation thing is so crazy. Now somebody says a picture is going to cost $10 million. A few years ago I would have had to sit back and say, "Well, I don't know if I want to get involved in something that big." That's not big any more.

But I have very strong feelings that any good film today that costs between $5 million and $10 million—that there's no reason in the world you cannot let it at least pay for itself. But these guys want to take it down the middle. They don't realize that there's a market for everything today in this country. *Being There* looks like it's going to be a successful film. And it isn't down the middle—not that that doesn't come into it. But you should never gauge it. You should never say,

"That's where I'm going to aim my film." Who in the hell wants to aim a film down the middle? Is that what you make a film for? For the middle of the road?

You don't make your films for that. You make your films for a reason. What guides me are my instincts—what I feel about something. It's the only thing I know, and so I have to rely upon that—that what I know as these instincts are going to affect a number of people. That's all any of us have. So go for what you're going for and find that.

Hal Ashby: Satisfaction in *Being There*

Jordan R. Young and Mike Bruns/1980

From *Millimeter*, May 1980. Reprinted with permission of Penton Media.

The films of Hal Ashby, from the wild and free-spirited *Harold and Maude* to the emotionally devastating *Coming Home*, are fresh and original. They reflect a unique sense of humor, a profound outlook on life and, above all, a deep-rooted humanity. Deciding that the development and production of his films took far too long, the director embarked on an experiment in 1978 to speed up the process. He shot two films back to back and then edited them simultaneously. The result: *Being There*, and the upcoming *Second Hand Hearts* (originally titled *The Hamster of Happiness*). Ashby took time out to discuss his latest work, his future plans, and his views on filmmaking in a recent interview at his house in Malibu, California, at the edge of the Pacific Ocean.

MM: You first read *Being There* several years ago, didn't you?

HA: Yes. Peter Sellers brought me the book in 1973. I'd just finished shooting *The Last Detail*. We couldn't get it together then, and Jerzy Kosinski wasn't willing to let it go. I think he might've, I don't know—he never really got tested. He said he would let go of it, that we could do it, we just never got far enough to offer him the money. Peter and I were never at a place where anybody would give us the money to make a real offer to the man.

MM: How did it suddenly materialize as a film?

HA: About two years ago I was sitting here and Andy Braunsberg walked in. He didn't know the history of the project. He said, "Would you be interested in doing this thing called *Being There*?" I said, "Absolutely. But I wouldn't do it with anybody but Peter Sellers." I'd never visualized it any way, ever, except with him. I don't think Jerzy was so hot for him, strangely enough. I remember Ryan O'Neal was mentioned to me at one point. The book describes more physically that kind of person, but I don't know how he ever could've made it work.

MM: Didn't Robert Jones work on the adaptation with Kosinski?

HA: No. What happened was, Jerzy's script, for my taste, was too heavy-handed. There's a certain thing that can happen with people when they don't make films, and it's understandable. I was in El Paso shooting *Hearts* and I had Robert come down; Jerzy had made a second pass at it and I had Andy Braunsberg sitting with him. I didn't have the time, first of all, and I didn't feel as comfortable sitting with the author and going through that kind of thing, having a lot of dialog about why it was this and why it was that, which is all good—it's always good to have information—but I felt he was fighting it in his scripts. It could have been that he was away from the book for so long—if you go back and you look at your film six years later, you say, "Well, I think I could do this . . ."

Also, it looked to me like Jerzy was a little afraid of the character he had drawn in Chance, in the book. He was afraid of him being a total retard. So I gave Robert Jones the book, and I gave him Jerzy's screenplay, and I asked him to write the script. A few weeks later he gave me a screenplay, and I knew I was into the film then. I'd always felt strongly about it being a film, but now I had my blueprint, my structure there. Then I sat down with Robert for three or four weeks and we worked really hard on it, eight or nine hours a day. We never worked with Jerzy on the script; when we sent it to him, he loved it.

MM: As it is, the film is very close to the book.

HA: Absolutely. There's another ending Robert wrote, which is great. Chance leaves the funeral, and Eve goes after him; he's doing a little thing with this tree, using his umbrella as a windscreen to protect it, and she says, "Where were you? I was looking for you." And he says, "I was looking for you, too, Eve." That was the way it ended. We were down in Asheville, North Carolina, and I was sitting and thinking about what was going on with the film. I was talking with Rudy Wurlitzer about how it had come to life, how Peter was playing it, how the innocence of the childlike character was coming through so strong and how the other actors were responding to it. I said, "I could just have him walking on water at the end." And I thought, "I'm going to have him walking on water."

MM: Are you saying that we make our own reality?

HA: It was interesting to see the different reactions when I said I was going to do that. Somebody said, "I don't know about him walking on water." I said, "Why?" He said, "You know what that means." "What?" "There's only one person who can walk on water." I said, "Well, I don't know . . ." I did it basically for that reason, that there would be a lot of answers to it. If I could have had him walking just above the water, though, that would've made me happy.

MM: Once you have the script down and you go into pre-production, who do you work with and how do you work with them?

HA: When I start pre-production, the person I work closest with is my production designer, Michael Haller. He will have more ideas than anyone—especially on this one because when I shot the two pictures back to back I didn't use him on *Hearts*, I just let him go on *Being There*. We wanted sort of a special look and I didn't want anything to interfere with that. So I said, "Mike, all that's going to be on you." By the time I finished *Hearts*, he was so full of ideas—that's how the ghetto scene came about. He said, "When I was in Washington, D.C., I was looking around in the ghetto. It was real interesting." I just flashed on that. I said, "Oh, God, Chance has just *got* to come out there." I work real closely with Mike. When I start pre-production, he is the man that has the most information.

MM: How did you work with Caleb Deschanel to determine the visual style of the film?

HA: You sit down and you start talking about what that film is, and looking at the locations . . . it's really difficult to do, to talk about what it is that you want in that visual style. Also, it has to do with knowing someone's work, and I was very familiar with Caleb's work. I've known him since he was a student at USC. The way I usually approach it is, I ask the cinematographer what he's thinking about. Instead of going in and saying, "Let's do this, I want this . . . ," I say, "What do you think?"

MM: So instead of telling your DP what you want, you ask him how he sees it?

HA: Yeah, I start to feel it out and find out, because otherwise you cut off ideas too fast. The great thing about film is, it really is communal. It is *the* communal art. And you don't lose anything—all you do is gain. Your film just gains and gains. The more input you can get, the better it is.

MM: Did Peter Sellers have trouble staying within the rigid confines of that character?

HA: No. It was hard work, but he never had any trouble. The hardest part of it was actually the delivery of the lines; to make him sound childlike, and not make them sound like bad readings. It was a real fine line.

MM: It's so tremendously underplayed. Did you exercise much restraint on him?

HA: I never once had to hold Peter back. The only times we went too far were from Melvyn Douglas's ideas. He would be further out with the ideas—not that they were bad ideas, he had a great sense of humor. We would try and shoot them and they would be a bit too far out.

MM: What's your shooting ratio, on the average?

HA: About 30 to 1, I would think. I don't think it ever gets less than that. It may be 40 to 1 at times.

MM: As a director, how much freedom do you give your editors on the first cut?

HA: I give them complete freedom. I don't even hang around; I just let 'em go. Amy Jones went through four of five cuts of *Second Hand Hearts*. I looked at different cuts and made a couple of comments, really minor things. I sat down with both Amy and Don Zimmerman (*Being There*) the end of May, and I didn't look at either of the films until the end of September. In that period, I wasn't physically cutting myself; I would sit with the editors and talk with them about it. On *Being There*, when it got down to the last stages, the last six or seven weeks I physically sat and cut the film myself because I didn't have the time to transfer the thoughts to Donny. At that point, I knew I better physically do it, and have him sitting there with me. I don't think my physically doing it made any difference; it was out of necessity. The last few weeks it really got crazy; I would not be gone from that editing room any more than four hours any given time, seven days a week.

I'm going to edit on tape from now on. I'm building a very sophisticated computerized tape editing machine. The possibilities you can explore! The first time you look at your dailies you can punch a button and it's on another thing over here, and you haven't cut into anything. At the end of three or four hours, you've got thirty minutes of selected takes which you haven't had to physically take out and move over there. But I don't think editing on tape will save me any time, because I'll use the time going after different thoughts and ideas.

MM: Are you completely satisfied with *Being There*, or could you continue to work on it?

HA: Oh, I'm sure I could. I could work on any of them. It's an ongoing process, but I'm not going to go back and re-cut them. After a film is out in the theater for a while, I don't go back and look at it anymore. I did see *Harold and Maude* again recently, and it was more damn fun . . . I had a lot of little surprises: "I didn't know I left that in."

MM: Did you make many changes in *Second Hand Hearts*, or did you film Charles Eastman's original script pretty much as it was?

HA: Pretty much as it was. The script had been around a long time. Charles had a thing about it—he wanted to direct it—and I knew that; we'd talked about it for years. Robert Blake finally bought it. He had somebody go up to his door and offer him cash. I couldn't get Eastman involved in the film. It was a pretty hard battle. I felt pretty much obligated at that point to go as much with that script as I possibly could. I changed very little: I didn't sit down with it myself and work on it. I just went with it; it was a script I liked a lot. But I wouldn't normally do that, and I'm not sure I would do it again. The biggest limitation I had was with Barbara Harris. I knew right away I would be limited in my editing with Barbara, but what she does is fantastic.

MM: With Blake, was there a conscious attempt to get away from the image he established in *Baretta*?

HA: I would think it was conscious on his part. I never talked with him much about it. Blake was very much into the character when we started shooting. Some people can't get rid of the macho thing in Blake; I think he completely lost it. He took chances in that film—I've never seen actors take chances like that. I let it go and get as crazy and as big as it could get.

MM: *Second Hand Hearts* doesn't seem very commercial. Does it to you?

HA: Yeah, it does. I don't know, though, because it's really about two people that are at the end of their ropes, and I'm not sure how much that appeals to people.

MM: Isn't it a rather offbeat choice, after the powerful drama of *Coming Home*?

HA: I don't think about things that way—what this does in relation to that.

MM: How are you going to promote *Second Hand Hearts*? Do you make those decisions?

HA: I'm making more of those decisions all the time. I don't want to leave it up to other people anymore. I don't think they know how to do it. One of the things I want to do in my advertising—and it's a very fine line—but I think film is one of the things you can advertise in this life and be honest about. If thoughts enter your mind that are not honest to that film, get rid of them. I want people to know there's humor in *Second Hand Hearts*; it isn't just a downbeat thing. The characters that Robert and Barbara play are crazy damn people, too.

MM: That was a nice campaign for *Being There*, that white-on-black silhouette that appeared in the papers.

HA: If you knew the fight I've had! Not only is it complicated with Lorimar, but it's doubly complicated because they have a contract with United Artists to release the picture—more people involved with it, that you have no contract with. The first ad ever run for *Being There* was a full page ad in *Variety*, for a pre-screening for Academy members, when I was working so crazy and hard on it. I didn't even know there was an ad—*nobody* had told me—and it was the worst thing I've ever seen in my life. I've never found out to this day who made up the ad. So I said, "That's it." I'm at a point where I'm not going to deal with these people anymore.

I'm at the point right now, fortunately, if I just wanted to make my own films, I could distribute them myself. I'm starting this company with Andy Braunsberg, Northstar International. I've always wanted to have a company, because I want to help young filmmakers. It's stupid not to do it. And morally, you've got to do it. The studios don't have a clue, when it comes to new filmmakers. When they have little flurries, and they try new filmmakers, nine times out of ten what they do is listen to the guy that talks the fastest. And that isn't necessarily the guy that makes the best films. I want to set it up where the people will run it themselves; they do not have to come to me and say, "What do you think?" I want to see the money being used that way. I think it's of real value to do that; it's a chance to use what you've got.

MM: There's a real sensitivity and compassion in all of your films.

HA: It comes out of your life. It's just something I have. I was blessed, very early on—I don't know what it was, but I always had the capacity to see through things real fast, to sit and think about things—that's all it requires for any amount of empathy or compassion, if you sit and think for two minutes about the position of anybody in the world other than yourself, and what they might feel like.

MM: How is it that you exercise so little authority on a set—you seem so laid back, so casual—yet when you shoot, everything is so precise?
HA: I really am a stickler for detail. I'll just hang in; I have a great tenacity. I think that has to do with the other philosophy, of trying to get as much creativity out of people as you can, their own creative energies and efforts. I think that's part of what it is. I'm not laid back; there's a tremendous energy going on all the time. What are you going to accomplish by raising your voice? Even if you're striving for some tense thing in the film, getting the crew tense isn't going to help. I went through a period in my life where I argued about everything, and I found I wasn't getting much accomplished.
MM: Your next film is with Jon Voight, from a script he co-wrote?
HA: Yes, it's called *Lookin' to Get Out*. He's been working on it since *Coming Home*. It's a comedy about two gamblers. Jon's a great writer—if they're good actors, they're good writers—they hear so good. I'm not quite sure where we're going with it. In the end, I think it's a film about learning how to let go. After that I'm going to do *The Hawkline Monster* with Jack Nicholson. I bought the rights to Richard Brautigan's novel several years ago.
MM: You were also thinking about doing *Henderson the Rain King* by Saul Bellow, weren't you?
HA: Yeah. I'm also going to do that with Jack. We may even do *Henderson* first; I'm not sure. We'll have to wait and see.

Whatever Happened to Hal Ashby?

Dale Pollock/1982

From the *Los Angeles Times*, October 10, 1982. Los Angeles Times, Copyright © 1982. Reprinted with permission of the *Los Angeles Times*.

Hal Ashby is known in Hollywood as a classy film director. His best work, as demonstrated in *Shampoo*, Warren Beatty's sexual salon odyssey, and *Being There*, a telling fable about the influence of television that marked Peter Sellers's last great performance, is provocative and stylish.

Since he began making movies in 1970 with *The Landlord*, Ashby has been one of the most consistent directors working in Hollywood. Although all his films have been made for major studios, he has remained fiercely independent, working within the system without really being part of it.

But for the last three years, Hal Ashby seems to have disappeared. Since the successful premiere of *Being There* in late 1979, two of the films he has made—*Second Hand Hearts* and *Lookin' to Get Out*—have failed to gain a national release. There have been ugly rumors that Ashby was in ill health, burned out by drugs, incapable of completing a movie.

And a director whose movies always enjoyed critical if not box-office success has been the victim of particularly damning reviews for *Lookin'* and its predecessor, *Second Hand Hearts*, which was released in 1981 for less than two weeks in only six cities.

There is an image in *Lookin' to Get Out*, Ashby's ninth film, that poignantly summarizes his plight. Jon Voight and Burt Young play two New York hustlers, and during an argument, Young turns on the TV set. Ashby appears on the screen, as if he might be on a talk show—but there is no sound. Voight turns off the set and Ashby disappears. Young turns it back on, but Ashby remains silent, spouting words that no one can hear.

Even Ashby agrees that these have not been the best of times for him. No one has heard what he has to say because hardly anyone has seen his films.

"This has been as heavy a period in my life as I ever want to have," the bearded wispy-haired film maker said in a recent series of interviews at his Malibu home and a Hollywood sound studio where he was mixing his latest film, *Time Is on Our Side*, a documentary (due for release next February) of the 1981 Rolling Stones concert tour.

Ashby recalled a recent conversation that he had with his old friend Jack Nicholson, who also starred in his 1973 film, *The Last Detail*. Nicholson told him, "You know, some people think you're dying." Ashby responded with his peculiar, high-pitched, maniacal laugh. "Dying?" Ashby asked, incredulous. "Yes!" shouted Nicholson. Ashby reflected for a moment. "I never got swamped by so much damn work in my life," he explained, "but I didn't know it killed me."

Hal Ashby is alive and well in Malibu. His gaunt face and sunken cheeks show the ravages of more than his fifty years. But he is vigorous, alert, and energetic, dressed in loose-fitting clothes and a rumpled blue corduroy jacket with elegantly embroidered dragons on the sleeves.

Ashby claims that he hasn't disappeared, he isn't dying, and, rather than being unable to complete a film, he has finished four in four years, an output that few other contemporary Hollywood directors have equaled. As for the drug rumors, Ashby says the accusations stem from his admitted marijuana smoking. "I hear all this stuff, but I personally don't get alarmed." Ashby explained, "As I go on with my life, I can't recall the last thing I heard about myself that was true."

Ashby almost invites gossip, however, by secluding himself in his Malibu Colony cottage that would look more comfortable on Cape Cod or his nearby offices, where he has set up a complex and expensive video editing system. And his decision to shoot two films back to back, then edit them simultaneously, backfired. He was forced to rush *Being There* into release just four months after he finished filming it, while *Second Hand Hearts* (originally titled *Hamster of Happiness*) took him almost two years to complete.

Ashby won't even go to see the version of *Lookin' to Get Out* now playing in theaters. Jon Voight, who co-wrote the story about a scam artist who flees to Las Vegas to avoid the Mob, also stars in the film and originated the project. He edited fifteen minutes out of Ashby's two-hour film, with the director's permission, if not his approval.

In any form, *Lookin'* has failed to attract an audience—Paramount Pictures reports that the movie sold only $500,000 worth of tickets in its first four days in three hundred theaters. And the critical reaction seems to be savage.

All this, Ashby claims, does not perturb him. He's happy to be isolated from Hollywood: "I see people there start to fall into the wrong things. They start living their lives on simple levels where they don't know the difference between right and wrong."

He is bitter about his experiences with Lorimar Films, the TV company (*Dallas*) that tried to make a big splash in movie production on the strength of a three-picture deal with Ashby. *Being There* was the company's biggest hit both here and abroad, but the relationship soured over fights between Ashby and Lorimar executives over the film's advertising campaign. It hit rock bottom when Lorimar, without informing Ashby beforehand, sold *Second Hand Hearts* and *Lookin'* to Paramount Pictures, which has not released them with great enthusiasm.

Ashby also accuses Lorimar of preventing him from directing *Tootsie*, the Dustin Hoffman-in-drag film, by notifying Columbia Pictures that he had not finished *Lookin'* or *Hearts* on time. (Sydney Pollack was eventually chosen to direct *Tootsie*.) Ashby, usually genial and friendly, can barely suppress his rage as he talks about the dispute.

"Nobody was more unhappy than I about the delays," he explained. "I'm not crazy—I would have liked nothing better than to look at *Second Hand Hearts* and think it was great. But I didn't, so I ended up putting a load on myself. And instead of getting help in the form of support from Lorimar, I got BS encouragement that you don't even waste your time listening to because you know it's not sincere."

Lorimar President Lee Rich said of Ashhy's complaints, "They're all ridiculous. Why even dignify them by answering them? They deserve no answer." Filming *Lookin' to Get Out* in Vegas while he was trying to edit *Hearts* and plan his Rolling Stones documentary was too much even for a workaholic like Ashby. "These last couple of years have been an especially hard time for me," Ashby says with a sigh. "I've run into more frustration than I could ever imagine. It's made me think about things I usually don't think about."

"I have actually been on the verge of amok my whole entire life."
—Loyal Muke, *Second Hand Hearts*

What Hal Ashby doesn't like to dwell on is his life before he became a Hollywood editor in 1963, and then a director seven years later with *The Landlord*, starring Beau Bridges and Pearl Bailey.

Raised in Ogden, Utah, during the depths of the Depression, Ashby felt an early sense of alienation as a non-Mormon in a predominantly Mormon state. His parents' twenty-five-year marriage broke up when he was five; when he was twelve, his father committed suicide. Ashby became a drifter, hitchhiking around the West, doing odd jobs, always reading books. In the fall of 1950, he was building railroad trestles in northern Wyoming when he went to get a drink of water. There was an inch of ice in the water barrel, prompting Ashby to announce to his co-workers, "I'm going to live off the fruits of the land."

He hitchhiked to the corner of Vermont and Santa Monica and took a seven-dollar-a-week room on Bunker Hill, working as a salesman for everything from magazines to encyclopedias. He didn't last long at any of the jobs. "You were always doing a con, telling a lie." Ashby explained. "I don't like to tell lies."

A job at Republic Studios running a multilith press led him to the studio's editing rooms. He was lucky enough to become apprenticed to Robert Swink, editor for director William Wyler, with whom he worked on *The Children's Hour*. Eventually Ashby became director Norman Jewison's editor, winning an Oscar for his cutting of *In the Heat of the Night*. Finally, Jewison gave him a chance to direct *The Landlord* and Ashby was on his way.

Since then, there has been a Hal Ashby film out every two or three years: *Harold and Maude* in 1971, with Bud Cort and Ruth Gordon as unlikely lovers; *The Last Detail* in 1973, with Jack Nicholson as a career sailor; *Shampoo* in 1975, starring Beatty as the philandering haircutter; *Bound for Glory* in 1976, the Dust Bowl–era film about folksinger Woody Guthrie with David Carradine in the title role; and the peak of Ashby's career, the pivotal antiwar movie *Coming Home* in 1978, for which he was nominated for an Academy Award.

Unlike other directors in the 1970s, Ashby never collected a cult reputation around himself. *Shampoo* is thought of as a Warren Beatty film; *Coming Home* was credited more often to producer and star Jane Fonda than director Ashby.

"That's all right, it doesn't bother me at all," Ashby said in his low, muttering voice. "If it did, I could do something about it very easily. I could be very blatant and play the role. But I honestly believe that film is a very communal art. People get out of it what they give to it."

At the beginning of his career, Ashby worried that his self-effacing attitude would reduce his own influence on his films. "But I didn't have to worry," he said. "The first time I saw a piece of film I directed, I realized all of me was in it."

Ashby put a lot of himself into films like *Bound for Glory* and *Second Hand Hearts*, a bittersweet love story about two of society's rejects played by Robert Blake and Barbara Harris. As Loyal Muke and Dinette Dusty, Blake and Harris offer an alternately infuriating and touching portrayal of human flotsam. (One of Harris's children in the film is named Human, a silent, withdrawn boy who seems a painful evocation of Ashby's own childhood.)

When Lorimar executives saw the film, according to Ashby, they didn't know what to do with it. Neither did Paramount Pictures, which opened the film in New York and Texas for a week in May 1981, and another week in Los Angeles and four other cities. There was no television or radio advertising, and no advertising at all in newspapers for the film's Boston run. Paramount wouldn't even screen the film in advance for critics.

The experience was particularly painful for Ashby, who had re-edited *Hearts* several times while working on his other films. Lorimar had hired a new editor to implement Ashby's changes, but the editor ended up changing the entire picture.

"It was a mess," Ashby conceded. "I basically have a very positive philosophy on life, because I don't feel I have anything to lose. Most things are going to turn out OK. But when I saw (the re-edited version) of *Second*, for the first time in my life I thought someone was ruining my picture."

It was only the latest in a series of disappointments Ashby had with Lorimar. He joined the company in 1978, after receiving assurances of creative freedom in making his movies, and control over who would distribute them. "That was one of the key appeals to me as a film maker," Ashby said. "It always hurts me to do battle over the marketing of my films. I have a pretty good idea of what I'm trying to say, and one of the goals of marketing is to convey some idea of that so people will go to see the film."

After working twenty-four-hour days to complete *Being There* in time for Christmas 1979 and Academy Award consideration, Ashby found that his preferred advertising campaign was abandoned. Lorimar's new campaign emphasized the love story between Peter Sellers as Chauncey Gardiner, the dim-witted political savant, and Shirley MacLaine, the wife of aging politician Melvyn Douglas (who won a best supporting Oscar for his role).

"They created a lie," Ashby says of Lorimar's ads. The former encyclopedia salesman has no more use for lies now than he did then. "They were trying do make it seem as if there was this tremendous love story because people like to go to see movies about men and women. But that's not what this picture was about."

Ashby said his final falling out with Lorimar came when he inquired about the radio ads for *Being There* in New York City. Lorimar Chairman Merv Adelson asked Ashby why he wanted to know. "Nobody listens to the radio in New York," Ashby recalls Adelson telling him. Ashby was dumbstruck.

"The first thing I wondered was if he was kidding me. Then I found out he was serious. He's a busy man and thinks, 'I don't listen to the radio in New York.' But he doesn't listen to the radio anywhere. He's not a radio listener. That's OK. There are lots of people who don't. That's part of life. But don't tell me *no one* listens to the radio." Although it hardly seemed as if the relationship between Ashby and Lorimar could deteriorate any further, *Second Hand Hearts* proved otherwise. Although Lorimar was well aware of his unusual plan to shoot two movies back to back and then edit them simultaneously, the company soon lost patience with the director. Rumors began to circulate through Hollywood that Ashby was incapable of finishing *Hearts*.

Not so, Ashby claims. "Editing two films at once was an interesting process that I shun now only because of the horrifying Lorimar experience," he said. "I was in one room editing *Being There* and concentrating heavily on that, but sometimes I just couldn't get it. Then all I had to do was get up, walk down the hall and into a room where they were working on *Hearts* and I'd get as involved in that as I was on the other film. That was the whole idea, and it worked very well."

Unfortunately, *Second Hand Hearts* didn't work quite so well. Ashby spent weeks tinkering with the movie, changing entire sections and replacing them with new footage. Finally, in May of 1980, he arrived at a version he liked, left detailed notes on how it should be constructed, and drove all night to Las Vegas where he began filming the next day on *Lookin' to Get Out*.

Again without his knowledge, Ashby claimed, Lorimar sneak-previewed *Hearts* to disastrous results. The director claims that the research companies hired by the studios attract what amounts to a cult sneak preview audience, older film patrons who attend only studio previews in selected cities. Based on the research, more changes were made by the time Paramount released the film the following year (supposedly as a contractual requirement to get a TV sale). Ashby had, in his words, "emotionally cut loose from the film."

Abandoning a film is a painful process for any film maker, but Ashby had to suffer through it not once but twice. He has declined to see the version of *Lookin' to Get Out* now playing across the country because it's not his version. "I directed it, it's a Hal Ashby film," the director said. "I made the decision to allow what (Jon Voight) did to the cut. I choose not to see it, not because I disagree with the cut, but because I don't want to second-guess him."

Ashby and Voight's relationship was a close one, going back to the intensity of filming *Coming Home*, in which Voight played a paraplegic veteran. But Ashby said he will never turn over one of his films again for someone else to edit.

"It's my responsibility. I can't negate that by saying, 'Hey, if they don't like it, it's your fault, not mine.' That's bull. I'm the one who said, 'OK, do what you want,' instead of 'No. I'm sorry. The version I have here is my cut, it's my film and I don't care what any of you think.' From now on, that's what I'm going to say."

To soothe his wounds, Ashby threw himself into the filming of *Time Is on Our Side*, a documentary of three Rolling Stones concerts that is as direct as the famous rock group's music. Ashby and Mick Jagger had long been friends and mutual admirers of each other's talents, and Ashby accepted immediately when the Stones offered him the opportunity to make the first major concert film since Martin Scorsese's *The Last Waltz* in 1978.

"I wanted a classical look, not a hand-held," Ashby explained. "I wanted to stay on a shot as long as could. This film has energy just from watching the Stones."

Embassy Pictures, the studio recently bought by Norman Lear and Jerry Perenchio, will release *Time Is on Our Side* in February, although not in the manner Ashby originally planned. He wanted patrons to be able to "jump up and down and holler" while watching *Time* in concert halls, not movie theaters. Embassy will employ a more traditional approach, however.

Never one to remain idle, Ashby is negotiating to direct a new Diane Keaton film, *Modern Bride*, which the actress will co-produce with Richard Roth (*Julia*) for Orion Pictures. Two of his more expensive projects, a film version of Gore Vidal's apocalyptic novel, *Kalki*, which will star Mick Jagger, and a cinematic adaptation of Richard Brauntigan's Gothic mystery, *The Hawkline Monster*, are in limbo while Ashby tries to figure out how to make them cost less.

For now Ashby is just trying to recuperate from the tensions and trials of the last four years. Or as Loyal Muke put it, "You just got to learn to take the bitter with the better. That's my philosophy."

"Directed by William Wyler" Interview

Scott Berg/1985

Unpublished interview conducted on February 12, 1985. Reprinted with permission of Catherine Wyler.

Scott Berg: How did you first meet William Wyler?

Hal Ashby: Well, I first met Willy Wyler when I was like the fifth assistant editor—the apprentice editor, in short—on a picture he directed called *The Big Country*. I had worked in different jobs. It was the first big picture that I really went on to, and I think I went on to it because I was a good hard worker. Bob Swink was the chief editor on it, and whenever they finished working on a reel everybody would go down to the cutting room, and it was a little speech that Mr. Wyler made [laughs] to me as being the last person on the picture. And he asked me, "Whenever you have any ideas about anything in the reel at all, any cuts in the reel, please get them out some way. Find some way to bring what it is that you have to say." I had never been asked my opinion before [laughs]—that's part of what goes on in the cutting room. I think of him so tenderly that way because he opened up all those doors for me. He made me think more creatively than I had in my whole life. I mean, it was just an attitude towards how they would look at film, so I met him on that picture in that particular way. He also said, "It's fine if I tell you that's a lousy idea, [laughs loudly] and it's crazy, and I'm real hard on you. It doesn't mean that I don't want to hear the ideas; it just means that arguments tend to sound personal." [laughs loudly] That's how he put it, and he said, "So, please, get them out."

Now I can also remember a little later date one time when he was asking my opinion about something in the projection room. While he was asking me, and I was rambling on a little like I am right now, he had some little thing in his hand that he kind of wore like with a watch fob thing, and he kept spinning it. [laughs loudly] He looked down at it, he was spinning it, what it did was to spin real fast and you could read what it had on it and it said, "Piss On You." [laughs loudly] Needless to say, I don't know how he took my thing. That was how I met him, that was my first introduction.

Scott Berg: Now were there specific things you came up with?

Hal Ashby: Gosh, I don't even remember. I mean, most of my ideas of the time I don't think they sounded so hot [laughs loudly] because I really didn't know very much. But I must say, the main thing was that he was always willing to listen to the idea, he really did *mean* it, he meant that's how good films are made. And he said, "That's why you've got to get it out." And he meant, "And when I do yell at you and holler at you, I really *don't* mean that. I don't mean it. I don't mean that you're stupid or you're dumb," he said, "because you must struggle to get things out because that's how good films *are* made." Ideas I may have had I wouldn't remember right now, and there are so many that go around.

Scott Berg: What other films did you do under his baton?

Hal Ashby: Well, I worked on that one. One nice thing, when you worked with Wyler, you worked for a long time. [long laugh] I worked a lot with the editor that he worked with for such a long time, which was Bob Swink. The other film that I worked the longest was *The Children's Hour*.

I remember so many things because in the editorial you come into such contact all the time. I meant that I as an assistant, you know, would spend so much time personally with him and so forth. I could go on for hours [laughs] about the things that would happen with him. I still to this day, my notepaper at home has to do with . . . If I ramble on and digress, if you want me to stop, please do . . . I have my notepaper at home which I told somebody about. I think it was on *Big Country*, and we went on a preview down in Long Beach. And we got back about one o'clock in the morning, we got back to the Goldwyn Studios, and we were up in his office. We were all talking about things, and all during the discussions, he was sitting at his desk and he just kept doing something on a pad of paper. When we left, after we'd been up there talking for about an hour, maybe two o'clock in the morning, I looked [laughs] at his desk to see what it was. And on this pad of paper, he'd just written the word "Decisions." [laughs] He just kept writing it over and over, [laughs] and had nothing else on the page at all. I remember telling a friend of mine about that about five years ago. [laughs] They had scratch paper, note paper, made up for me with this particular thing. That was, uh, oh God. [laughs]

I remember another thing also, another preview. When I went, there was such a big crew on *Big Country* that they couldn't take everybody. I was so into the film, they [were previewing in] San Francisco, and so I paid my own way up there, you know, and just went to the theater. Of course, when Willy saw me there, he said to make sure that I was paid and everything. One of the things I remember the strongest about that preview was that, I think on reel seven, it came up out of sync. [laughs] I found out something that night—I'm sure he already knew it. I found out how interested an audience was by how upset they got when they had to stop. But it was down for probably ten minutes because there were somebody's nervous fingers in there trying to thread up the negative and get it all back in sync and everything. And when I went back down in the projection room, a lot of people had come out to get candy and popcorn and so forth, and when they started the picture back up, there was Willy running around in the lobby grabbing people and saying, "The picture has started again, the picture has started again," *forcing* [laughs] them back into the theater! There was no question about it, he wasn't polite or anything, he was just grabbing them and throwing them back in! It was hysterical.

Scott Berg: In the cutting room, how involved was Wyler in the editorial process would you say?

Hal Ashby: Well, because of having Bobby Swink, he really left a lot up to Bobby. I mean, like when we actually did the finish of *The Big Country*, he was over shooting *Ben-Hur* and I remember Bobby taking one of the last prints—it may have even been the answer print—over to Willy in Rome to show him. But he would spent a lot of time in the projection room.

On *Children's Hour*, there was a point where he spent quite a bit of time in the cutting room. But because of that good relationship with Bobby—which is the relationship everybody *should* have with an editor—he didn't spend that much time directly over his shoulder. He utilized his time.

I've always wished I could find someone like Bobby as I'm directing now, because I think it helped Willy in his output of what he could do. He could get more pictures out. I looked, it was a long period of time when he had two a year coming out! It dawned on me how he did that [laughs]—it had to be with a good editorial staff.

Scott Berg: How much understanding do you think he had of the editorial process?

Hal Ashby: Oh, I think he had a good understanding of it. I think that Willy had a very good understanding of the editorial process. I never found him wanting for, you know, to try to figure anything out as far as the mechanics of it were, or how the machinations of it worked. The only thing that would be funny because of him not spending all that great amount of time in the room was some of the arguments he and Robert would get into, and they got into some *horrendous* [laughs] arguments.

On *Big Country*, for example, when we ran what we call the first cut, or the rough cut, which was three months after the picture was finished shooting, [laughs] it was like twenty-eight reels, first cut. At the end of reel fourteen, Bobby had put a piece of leader that said, "Place Commercial Here," figuring that they would take a break and [laughs] go have dinner. As I said, it was this huge crew, and I being the fifth assistant, the apprentice, I didn't go up to dinner with everybody. We were down at Goldwyn Room A, and I was waiting there for them, waiting there for them. About 11:30, one of the other editors came back, a man by the name of Bob Belcher. He came back and said, "What are you doing here?" I said, "Well, I'm waiting for them to come back. We finish running the picture. They've only run the first fourteen reels!" Willy had never seen the picture all the way through. And he said, "Oh, God, they aren't coming back!" I said, "Why?" He said, "Bob quit!" [laughs loudly] So they were discussing the first fourteen reels and apparently had this *huge* argument, and Bob walked out. But he was back the next day and continued on. Those are the kind of things that go on.

Scott Berg: We've noticed there is a certain fatness to Wyler's films in the '50s, when he became his own producer. Do think part of it was not having a Sam Goldwyn or a strong producer to rub against? Do you think there is some disadvantage to being your own producer-director?

Hal Ashby: I don't know, I guess. I assume from some of the things that Willy had told me—not told me, but that I heard . . . A good example of that is that [Samuel] Goldwyn was an exceptionally strong producer. I remember leaving the projection room one time—I think it was while working on *Children's Hour*—and we were going by the open booth. There was a couple of goldbergs that I noticed had *Wuthering Heights* on it. I just poked Willy and said, "Hey look, how about that?" I'm sure his mind was well into the other picture we had just come out of, and he said, "Oh, yes. You know I shot a much better ending than is on the picture." [Ashby cracks up laughing.] I was absolutely astounded. I said, "What do you mean?" and he proceeded to tell me. I don't remember exactly what it was that happened, but he did say that Goldwyn didn't like the ending that Willy had had on the picture and that he had had another ending shot for the picture. My God, that's absolutely amazing, because I'm sure at the time it must have cost a tremendous amount of [money]. I just remember it as, first of all, it startled me, and then it made me also see how strong a person that Goldwyn was, and then it also showed me that there was an incredible thing about how you get over something, in other words, how at a later time you can not have the . . . Because it didn't bother Willy, he just said it, as a matter of fact, like, "Oh sure, that went on," and so forth. As to whether it made his pictures better, I'm not sure.

But I think he was very, very tough. I think if those films felt fat, they might have been the films themselves, what they were and how this filmmaking itself expanded in their stories. Like *Big Country* was a big, big picture. God, it was shot in Technorama, big like Vistavision, a big wide frame, and we had so much [footage]. According to Bobby, he always shot a lot of versions of things. He shot a lot of film, but he actually shot versions and versions, which was wonderful as an editor. It was just terrific, it gives you so many different ways to go. [laughs] But he left himself with a lot of latitude. I have a feeling he was always pretty strong with that.

Scott Berg: How would you describe the particular quality of his films?

Hal Ashby: I always thought of Willy as very based in reality, his films are based in reality. He had a great sense of humor that went along with things, and he'd get pretty much out there and so forth, but his base in reality always made him go after that which would never feel false. I felt I learned along the way from Willy that he didn't want to be untruthful. He had very strong feelings that way, and he would make films for reasons. I remember one time talking about *The Big Country*, a big, huge film that took all these people this long, long time to make it. One of the things he felt very strongly about it—I remember him talking to Bobby in the projection room one day. They had this fight sequence in it and it was wonderful. It was shot with these long shots that they did. In this fight between Charlton Heston and Gregory Peck, at the end of the fight, and where either man had exhausted themselves and beaten the hell out of each other, Peck had a line that said, "Now, tell me, Leach, what did we prove?" And that was one of the reasons for Willy making the film. He had these very honest things, very, very simple things sometimes, that would be basic drives, they would be reasons for him making these films, and so forth. And that reality came out of that, along with his incredible sense of humor that he had. As tough as he could get—[laughs] I saw him put a couple of people in tears before!—there was always that base of reality that was so good.

Scott Berg: Let me ask you one more question about *The Big Country*. You said he was off to do *Ben-Hur*. Had he hung around, do you think the picture would have been cut differently?

Hal Ashby: Well, I don't know, because he really had long, long sessions in the projection with Swink and the editors before he went off to do *Ben-Hur*. He wasn't happy with the ending, and Bobby went up and shot just an ending with Jean Simmons and Peck riding off down from this higher place coming from the mountains away from the camera together, and that was the only thing I could really think of that was done without Willy knowing it. I don't think he had any great surprises when Bobby took the picture back, when he took it over to him in Rome. I don't remember it as that way, at least. We had such long sessions and by the time he did leave, I remember we did a lot of long hours and a lot of pressure, wanting to get as much done before Willy took off.

Scott Berg: When Wyler was out of the room, what was the scuttlebutt among the editors about Wyler? What were the eccentricities, peculiarities, the inside dirt?

Hal Ashby: Well, I'm trying to remember because I went on with Swink from that picture; strangely enough, I ended up his assistant. Bobby might complain with other directors about what they shot or didn't shoot and so forth, but I don't remember him complaining that way with Willy. There was such a close relationship, they had such a good feeling. Bobby would tell me a lot of stories about Willy, and I can remember Bobby telling me a story about Willy from *Roman Holiday*, which to me is one of the most hysterical stories I've ever heard. But there apparently was a scene—they finished editing the film in Italy also—that Bobby didn't like, Willy did like. When they first came back to California to run the picture for the Paramount executives, Bobby told me that at the end of the screening everybody said, "Oh, my God, it's just wonderful. Awful pleased with the film," and so forth. And Willy proceeds to stand up and tell everybody, "Well, if you think it was wonderful . . ." and he describes this great scene which Bobby always said was never that good. Everybody asked, "Why isn't that in the picture?" and he said, "Because this man here"—and he points to Bobby—"doesn't want it in the picture. He didn't think it was any good." Now they all turned to Bobby and said, "How can you not have that scene in the picture, this wonderful scene?" I forget what the scene was—it doesn't matter—but Bobby, he said he'd had a feeling, so he had brought the scene with him when he came and had it in a can. He said, "I just happen to have it," and he ran it for everybody, and they all looked like they didn't like it. So they would have those kind of games, that's like Bobby telling stories out of school on Willy. That's the main thing, Bobby telling me more like anecdotes about things that happened with Willy prior to the time that I knew him and wasn't around for things like that and so forth. I think that, you know, I just always felt a deep affection for him, even though I saw him get into arguments that I couldn't believe, I've never been anywhere near before in my life or after in my lifetime.

Scott Berg: Is there such a thing as a Wyler style? Can you see a trademark? An imprint on a Wyler film that would distinguish them?

Hal Ashby: I'm sure there is a style of Willy's. I always thought it was because he had such great restraint. I mean, he always held back, he never hit it on the head all the time. A great example for me of showing how somebody would do something would be in *The Best Years of Our Lives*, which I had nothing to do with, it's just a film I've seen a number of times. When Fredric March first comes home and he and Myrna Loy get together, it's that long shot down the hall and there is so much emotion to it. He would do that continually, always holding back, holding back. I just felt I learned so much from that particular thing. I kept looking for that kind of thing, so I kind of thought about that as his style, but he made so many different kinds of films. I don't know if it's the style of being able to do that with great restraint, but it's a great way of injecting humor without forcing it. One of the things I remember, as far as Willy's humor, was in *Big Country* we had scene where Burl Ives came out to the edge of his porch and they brought his horse around and told him to get on the horse. I don't know if it was Chuck Connors or which one it was who brought it around, but it was too far away from him to get on the horse. He just stood there and looked at him, and it never got that big a laugh, it never worked that big in *Big Country*. And when I was watching *Ben-Hur* later, he does the same thing and it got a big laugh in that picture. I always thought that was a great thing: if it doesn't work in one way, I'll try it in another. I think if it had worked in the one he wouldn't have used in the other.

Scott Berg: You mentioned Wyler's influence on you just in terms of getting you to think creatively and in terms of film. What influence did he have on your career? Did he affect your becoming a director at all? Do you carry him around when you direct in any way?

Hal Ashby: Oh, I think I carry him around all the time when I direct, although I never had discussions with him about that. It all had to do with just the absorption of his work and being close enough at times to really see how it happens. It was that very strong attitude about being able to listen to what other people had to say, like the first thing I was hit with when Willy said, "Let us hear what you have to say." It's something that I've carried and I think it's the only way for me—it came directly out of that. I don't think, "Gee, what would Willy have done with this?" or "How would Willy have done that?" That doesn't ever even enter into my mind, but I'm sure it's there in the subconscious, at least it's such a strong influence. It was through Willy and Bobby that I learned what it meant to direct a film; I didn't have a clue before that. And what was good about it was bringing it up, making one talk about what their ideas and thoughts were. That's the creative process. Prior to that, I can remember an editor looking at me across the room and saying, "Now whatever they say, don't open your mouth. Don't you say a word." I said, "I wouldn't know what to talk about anyway." [laughs] Which I wouldn't have. But this, I learned what to talk about. I'm sure the first ideas I had were horrendous ideas, but the fact that I was encouraged to keep doing it, and then you start learning and you really do learn, it's amazing. That, plus just Willy's gift of what he did with his films. You know, it becomes an instinctive thing, like the restraint, holding back and so forth. I remember and think about those things very strongly, I think they are very important things in the films, and in that way I try to be the same way and think the same way.

Scott Berg: Now, I'm questioned out, unless you have anything else. Are there any other things you'd like to say?

Hal Ashby: Well, the things I remember about Willy and fighting, arguments. When I worked with Bobby Swink, I've never seen anybody have arguments—I mean never before I came into contact with him or after I left him and was out on my own—I've never seen anybody have arguments the way they had arguments. I mean, they were incredible. A good came out of them and I'm not sure if they were sometimes . . . I can relate one short story that had to do with *Big Country*, with the close-up of Charles Bickford at the end of it. Bobby had a long shot and in the projection room Willy would not let go of it. He said, "Didn't I shoot a close-up of that?" And Bobby said, "Yes." "Why?" He said, "I thought this was better." Fifteen minutes later, Willy would still be on it, we'd be off on another sequence and he would still be saying, "Well, how could anybody not put the close-up of the man in the last sequence of the picture?" And he'd go on and that was needling and so forth, but I saw them get in arguments and I saw Bobby throw a reel on the floor one time he was so angry and so furious with him and so forth. They would literally really yell at each other. And they maintained this wonderful relationship, they were close enough they could do that, I guess is what it is. They could do it.

How to Kill a Movie

Michael Dare/1986

From *LA Weekly*, May 16, 1986. Reprinted with permission of Michael Dare.

In Susan Seidelman's original ending for *Desperately Seeking Susan*, the two heroines brush off all the guys and run off together to Egypt; in Orion's version, they go back to their fellas. In Terry Gilliam's version of *Brazil*, there's a happy ending that turns out to be a cruel delusion; in Universal's version, the last shot was cut to keep the happy ending happy. Though *Brazil* is one of the few cases in which the filmmaker prevailed (Universal released Gilliam's cut), we'll never know what Adrian Lyne really had in mind when he made *9½ Weeks* or what Ridley Scott was imagining when he made *Legend*. Studios hacked those pictures to shreds in last-ditch efforts to make them more commercial.

Does anybody really think that *Desperately Seeking Susan* would have been *less* commercial with a more outrageous ending? Orion did—and obviously they're not alone. For as these (and many other) examples show, we're being inundated with pictures with no single guiding intelligence to guarantee that they make sense. They're nobody's version of anything, just bastardized "product" out to make a buck.

People often wonder how so much time and money can be spent on projects that seem to have been made by nobody. This is the story of what happened to one such bastardized movie, *8 Million Ways to Die*, a film disowned by its producer Steve Roth, its director Hal Ashby, and its stars, Jeff Bridges and Rosanna Arquette. With its cross-purposes, assembly-line methods, and battles between backers and artists, this production story provides a textbook example of how to kill a movie. It is one such story among many.

8 Million Ways to Die should have been a contender. The story was a thriller, but it was more than a thriller—it tackled the subject of addiction.

It started out as a hot property, a prizewinning crime novel by Lawrence Block about an alcoholic ex-cop and a coke-happy hooker in New York who fall in love despite the murderous interference of a drug-dealer named Angel. Like most hot properties it went through the standard Hollywood permutations. Screenwriter Oliver Stone (*Midnight Express, Salvador*) adapted the novel; and his script was originally slated to be directed by Walter Hill, with Nick Nolte in the starring role. As often happens, the project fell through.

The film took its present shape when producer Steve Roth set up a deal between PSO (Producers Sales Organization) and director Hal Ashby to shoot Stone's script with Bridges and Jamie Lee Curtis as leads; ultimately, Arquette replaced Curtis. Then Stone's script was thrown out when, for budgetary reasons, the setting was changed from New York to L.A. and Stone was too busy directing *Salvador* to rework the story.

Script-doctor supreme Robert Towne took over the job (he's uncredited) and worked to preserve the blend of addiction-study and thriller that made the story special. He even wanted to change the title to *Easy Does It*, an Alcoholics Anonymous slogan seen frequently on bumper stickers. In turn, AA was impressed by the filmmakers' sincere belief that they were creating a serious film about the spiritual aspects of battling alcoholism and drug addiction. For the first time, Alcoholics Anonymous actually allowed its name to be used in a film.

This seemed to be an optimistic and rather fitting sign, for rumors of chaos on the set and rampant drug-abuse had been attached to Ashby's last few pictures. And since *Second-Hand Hearts, Lookin' to Get Out*, and *The Slugger's Wife* had all been resounding commercial and critical failures—thereby fueling the speculation about drugs—some people had begun to ask whether Ashby was still capable of making a good film.

Towne completed about half the script before shooting began, leaving the actors a lot of room to improvise, a "hardship" they cheerfully embraced. Ashby, Arquette, and Bridges spent long afternoons in their trailers writing scenes. Soon word got out that the picture was in trouble. (There was even vague speculation as to what they all were *really* doing behind closed doors.)

All along, there, was pressure from PSO to get on with the production. Though the start-date kept getting pushed back, PSO decided not to adjust the release date. Tension on the set mounted. The fact that the script was being rewritten as they went along, and that Bridges and

Arquette felt free to participate actively in creating their characters, led to problems: PSO's completion-bond company wanted to see the actual pages of script before they were shot each day; but given Towne's constant rewriting and all the improvisation, the money-men couldn't see the script until *after* each day's shooting.

Once they had finished shooting, the real trouble began. Perhaps the PSO people thought they were losing control of the project, or that Ashby would take so long editing that *they* wouldn't have time to make their own final cut before release. In any case, two weeks after the last day of shooting, Ashby was fired from the picture and the actual negative was moved to another editing facility.

At first Ashby didn't take the firing seriously, deeming it just another ploy in the constant political shuffle of Hollywood filmmaking. Besides, he always lets his editor do a first cut with no interference, making his own cut only when the editor says it's ready. In this case, he handed the film over to his chosen editor, Robert Lawrence, and lounged on the beach for a couple of weeks, assuming that eventually PSO would let him do his own cut. (Ashby, after all, had made his name as a film editor, even winning a 1967 Oscar for *In the Heat of the Night*.) Instead, PSO hired editor Stuart Pappé (*An Unmarried Woman*) to do the editing and Lawrence quit (though he'd been invited to stay). Pappé never spoke to Ashby while editing the footage; indeed, Ashby still hadn't seen any of the film other than the dailies he saw while shooting.

Fights between producers and directors are not uncommon in Hollywood, but they're usually over artistic differences. "Why is it three and a half hours long and not in chronological order?"—that's the kind of thing one hears when studios catch their first glimpse of someone's latest "masterpiece." But that didn't happen here, and PSO said nothing of the kind, because Ashby was never given a chance to finish. There wasn't anything wrong *or* right about the Ashby version of *8 Million Ways to Die*—it only existed in his mind.

Nevertheless, this film with Ashby's name on it has been lambasted by most critics for its Miami vices: too much dirty language (fuck this, fuck that), too much sleaze, and an incoherently developed theme about alcoholism and drugs. Ashby says this isn't *his* film, that only he could possibly know how the pieces were supposed to fit together and he was never consulted during post-production.

Bridges and Arquette share the same sense of betrayal. Throughout his career, Ashby has been known as an actor's director and, in fact, has directed his actors to numerous Academy Award nominations (e.g., Jon Voight and Jane Fonda for *Coming Home*). Actors will take chances with him that they wouldn't necessarily take with anyone else. While shooting, he frequently gives them extra takes, allowing them to experiment, fool around, deviate from the script, hang loose, and take the chance of looking stupid—trusting that during editing, Ashby will use only the takes that make everyone look best. To fire Ashby was not just a surprising power maneuver but a considerable betrayal of the actors' confidence. Arquette, in particular, has received horrible notices but it's quite possible there's no single shot of her in the film that Ashby would have used.

Bridges's performance isn't exactly what Ashby had in mind either. Though it's considered the norm in Hollywood, Ashby doesn't believe in postdubbing (or "looping") the actors' voices. (Even in *Bound for Glory*, when David Carradine plays the guitar on the top of a moving train, you're hearing live sound.) After Ashby was fired, Bridges was given two hundred lines of dialogue to loop. In effect, more half of the audio version of his performance was directed by editor Stuart Pappé.

Ashby took PSO into arbitration at the Directors Guild under a DGA rule that if a director completes shooting, he or she has the inalienable right to a director's cut; the director is also given ten weeks for editing and a set number of previews. But TriStar, the film's distributor, planned to testify that it needed the film released in April because of a threatened movie glut in May. Normally, in that type of "expedited arbitration," the DGA cuts the editing time in half. For Ashby, the idea of five weeks of editing was laughable. He wanted to continue working toward the original April date. "It would have been silly to go for expedited arbitration and end up having to hand the film over unfinished. It would have been too frustrating. And there would have been nothing to stop them from releasing *their* version in the meantime."

As it turned out, PSO did release its version—to a shellacking from the critics and a lack of interest from the audience. Were it not for the film's box-office failure, the ruin of a once-promising project and the waste of time for all the talent involved, this story would have a happy ending. All potential litigation has been resolved. Ashby has been compensated for his removal from the picture. No one's reputation has been ruined. Arquette, Bridges, and Ashby are all working on new films. And PSO is now getting out of producing and sticking to distribution.

But not before having made some very strange choices and a lot of enemies.

ROSANNA ARQUETTE—ACTRESS (*The Executioner's Song, Desperately Seeking Susan, After Hours*)
"The only reason Jeff Bridges and I did the movie was because Hal Ashby was involved; and it was one of my greatest experiences working with him. He's a great actor's director; he's always there with you. The guy's an artist, a true, true artist. Hal lets you do your thing with a very strong guiding hand. He's in fine shape, better than he's ever been, but obviously they only hired him to get us. I guess they hired me because they wanted me to show my tits, I don't know. PSO was flipped out because I didn't do any nudity. Hal and I decided, 'Why do we have to show a hooker fuck?' . . .

"We'd purposely do takes where we'd overact, then calm down and do a take right after that was perfect. One example is when Jeff and I were riding down on the tram the first time. The way it is now, I say, 'Prick' and he says, 'Fucking cunt' and I say, 'Fuck you.' That was, just us on the first take warming up to get into it. Hal would never have put that in the movie . . .

"I go from a tough chick to suddenly I'm nice. It wasn't like that at all, and I'm getting attacked because they left all these scenes out. I was really proud of what I did in this movie. It was a completely different character from my others. But they made me look like a jerk, like I decided to play it that way, and I didn't. It's the most painful experience in the world to know that Hal didn't get to decide which takes to use.

"It's really scary considering how many people in Hollywood think you're only as good as your last film. I do this *for a living*. Besides our love of the work, it's the way we support ourselves. These people are fucking with my *life*. I had heard that the film was in terrible shape, but the only bad thing was them coming to the set and hovering with their bad vibes. Hal is clean, protective, energetic, and supportive. They come on with doom and blackness and time and money and pressure . . .

"They even have the score in *mono*. They wouldn't put up the extra $5,000 to have it in stereo. It's unbelievable! They took pieces of music written for one segment and put them in another. They even told James Newton Howard to rewrite the music more like *Miami Vice*. I said, 'You guys wanted to make *Miami Vice*, and instead you made *Miami Twice*.' Hal shouldn't see the film; it would kill him. It's a horrible, horrible thing . . .

"I mean, PSO thought they could edit the film better than Hal Ashby. What kind of mind thinks that way? Who do they think they are? Confiscating that film was the lowest thing anyone could do."

JEFF BRIDGES—ACTOR (*The Last Picture Show, Bad Company, Winter Kills, Cutter's Way, Starman, Jagged Edge*)

"I had one of the most creative times working on this picture I've ever had. Hal gave us space to create, and it wasn't just jerking off—we came up with good stuff. Unfortunately, they cut against the way Hal shot and conceived the film. He's one of the best directors I've ever worked with. He's an artist, though his process may look strange to people who aren't artists. They shouldn't have hired Hal in the first place if they wanted some other kind of film. We were going out of our way not to make a shoot-'em-up drug movie. There have been enough movies about drug dealers and cops . . .

"I was interested in exploring the obsessive side of his character. I went to AA meetings and found it to be an incredible organization, with an interesting perspective on how to live your life whether you're an alcoholic or not. I wanted to put some of that out. I wanted to explore the spiritual aspects of what an alcoholic goes through. It's a tricky subject to address in a movie, because when you talk about anything spiritual in a movie, there's a danger of getting too sappy or too preachy. We were very aware of that, and the scenes we shot dealing with it really walked that tightrope. They got the point across without being preachy. It's all been cut out of the film.

"I feel ripped around. In the first place, I did the picture to work with Hal. To have it pulled away at the stage where all his expertise lies—which is in the *editing*—made no sense to me whatsoever.

"Hal's magic lies in letting certain energies in. Some directors have it all planned out, but Hal is very open, and you'd be surprised the kind of things that just come in at the last moment. Hal's process is an exciting one, but I can see how it might be a little disconcerting for the money people. But they're big boys. They should know what moviemaking is all about. It wasn't as though they were unhappy with the parts of the film we were showing them. We were busting our butts, writing and shooting at the same time. I've never worked so hard on a picture in my life! We were locked in our dressing rooms writing our asses off. It's not like we were in there doing coke or anything. This was the cleanest, hardest-working set I've ever been on. I never saw anyone do anything . . .

"In the final film, they goosed up all the stuff we were trying to avoid. It was a case of fixing something that wasn't broken."

HAL ASHBY—DIRECTOR (*The Landlord, Harold and Maude, The Last Detail, Shampoo, Bound for Glory, Coming Home, Being There*)
"My experience as a director has always been that the moment you start directing that creative flow in somebody, you're doing them a disservice 99 percent of the time because you're throwing them off. It doesn't mean the creative flow stops, but all of a sudden they have to downshift and turn left instead of going straight ahead—just because you think you know the bridge is out. All you have to know is that if that person is creative, when they get to the bridge and it's out, they'll know it themselves. They won't need me to tell them. Just because they're brave doesn't make them stupid . . .

Everything concerned with *8 Million Ways to Die* was just my normal process. I know PSO had good reason to be anxious, but I'd never had people watching that close before. I don't know why. I've had them come up and say, 'Hey, you're five days behind,' and it's the normal thing, but this film had more of that than anything I've ever done. We finished the picture less than 10 percent over budget, which was well within the contingency estimated for completion. All of their comments during the making of the film were positive. They liked the dailies, and nobody complained . . .

"It's just a case of them not wanting me. Maybe they thought I wouldn't get it finished on time. I'm not quite clear. I've had these sort of situations before. With *Being There*, which only opened in two theaters on Christmas Day, I actually brought the film myself from the lab to the noon opening in L.A. That's how I look at editing. In this case, I don't even know what the arguments were. The wire that I got said that I was totally irresponsible and nonprofessional. I think they have to say that to fire you, but it's a little harsh when you've been working so hard . . .

"Once a director is removed, the danger is that there's this committee of editors who can't possibly think the same way. They offered me the opportunity to see the film to see if I wanted 'A HAL ASHBY FILM' on it—it was in my contract—but I couldn't look at it. I said obviously it's not "A HAL ASHBY FILM" unless *I* make it. I ended up with a payment, but what does that do? It doesn't give you your film. Talk about how experiences . . . "

MARK DAMON—EXECUTIVE PRODUCER (Founder, chairman, and former chief executive officer of PSO, which marketed *Das Boot, The Neverending Story, The Clan of the Cave Bear, 9½ Weeks,* and *Short Circuit*)

"I'm not a whimsical person. I don't operate on whims. What was done was done for a reason. I think I'm a total professional, and what was done was done with the best interests of everybody. Our firing Hal wasn't because we disagreed with or distrusted Hal's creative vision of the film. It was a business decision . . .

"I don't think there are many interpretations of this film. Ashby doesn't shoot a lot of footage, and he very much edits in camera. Therefore, any other editor coming on cannot, in my estimation, go very far afield from Ashby's intentions. It's not as though someone shot 500,000 feet of film and you had a year to assemble the pieces. If Ashby didn't want so much swearing in the movie, why did he print it in all those takes? . . .

"The man who was the final editor on the picture had long discussions with all the actors involved. I personally invited Rosanna and Jeff to make sure that their characterizations were reflected as much as possible in the film. They made comments to the editor, who made changes at their request. One scene about Arquette's background as a dancer was put back in because she wanted it. The scene made sense; it helped the character. I never wanted Arquette to do nudity. I left that decision up to the director . . .

"I knew that Hal was a very talented director, and when we hired Hal we hired a man whose talents we knew would eventually come out on the screen. I think the picture we eventually put into the marketplace was a picture that all parties can be proud of. In the end, I was satisfied with the product . . ."

STEVE ROTH—PRODUCER (Vice-chairman of ICM; packaged *Foul Play, Silver Streak, The Omen, Urban Cowboy, The Right Stuff.*)

"Hal is just great, and I loved the work he did. After he was fired, I didn't want to have anything to do with the film. The wrong takes were used, the wrong music was used . . . just a lot of dumb errors, and I blame myself for it. I put the whole thing together, and I never should have gotten involved with those guys at PSO. Hal Ashby and myself were trying to make a movie about an alcoholic, not so much about 'Hey, fuck you, Angel!'"

Index